Casper
the FRIENDLY GHOST

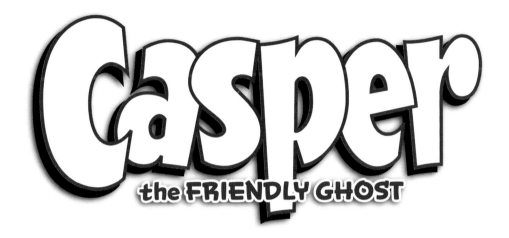

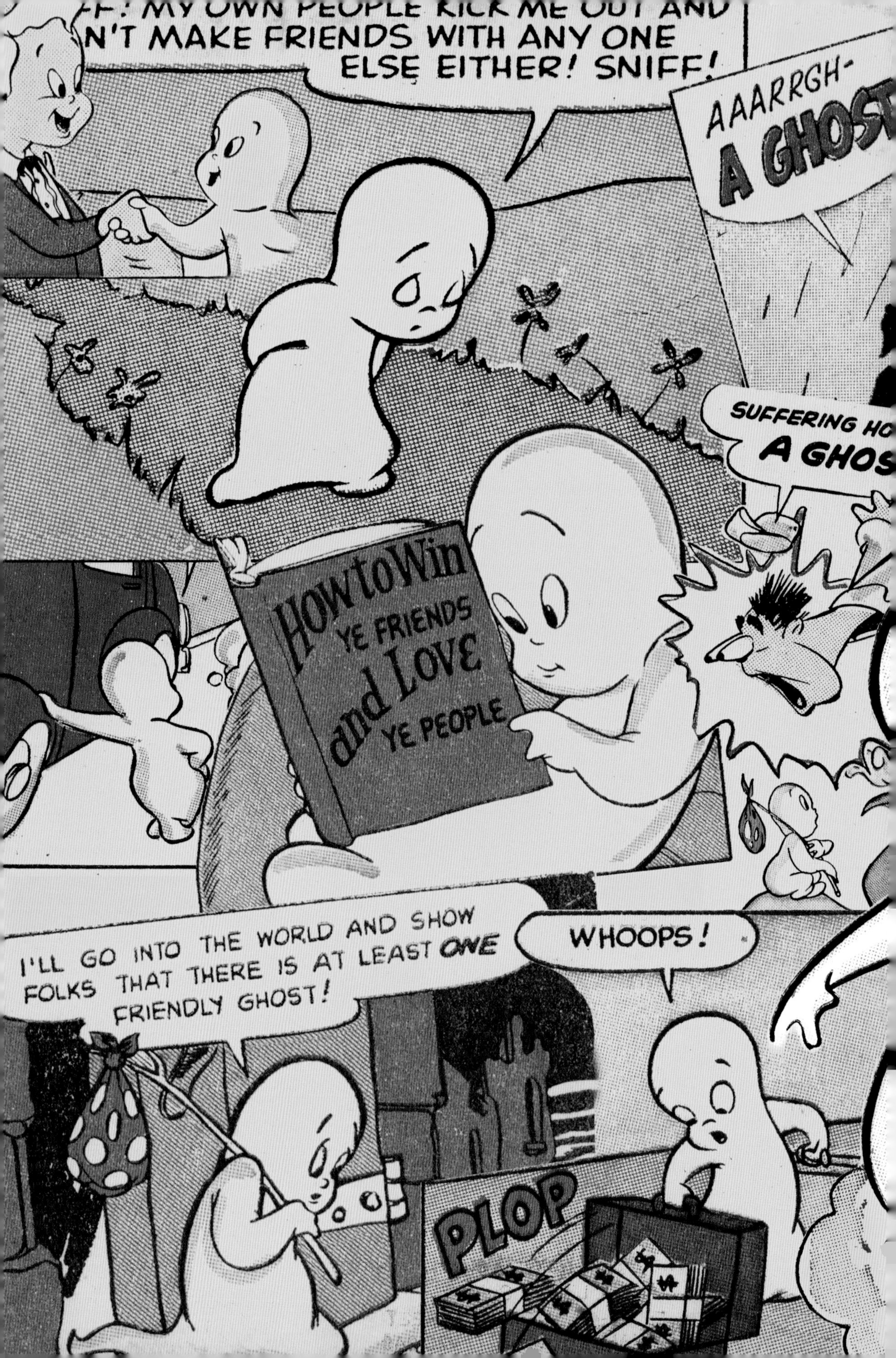

N'T MAKE FRIENDS WITH ANY ONE ELSE EITHER! SNIFF!
AAARRGH- A GHOST
SUFFERING HO A GHOS
HOW to Win YE FRIENDS and LOVE YE PEOPLE
I'LL GO INTO THE WORLD AND SHOW FOLKS THAT THERE IS AT LEAST ONE FRIENDLY GHOST!
WHOOPS!
PLOP

Casper®
the FRIENDLY GHOST

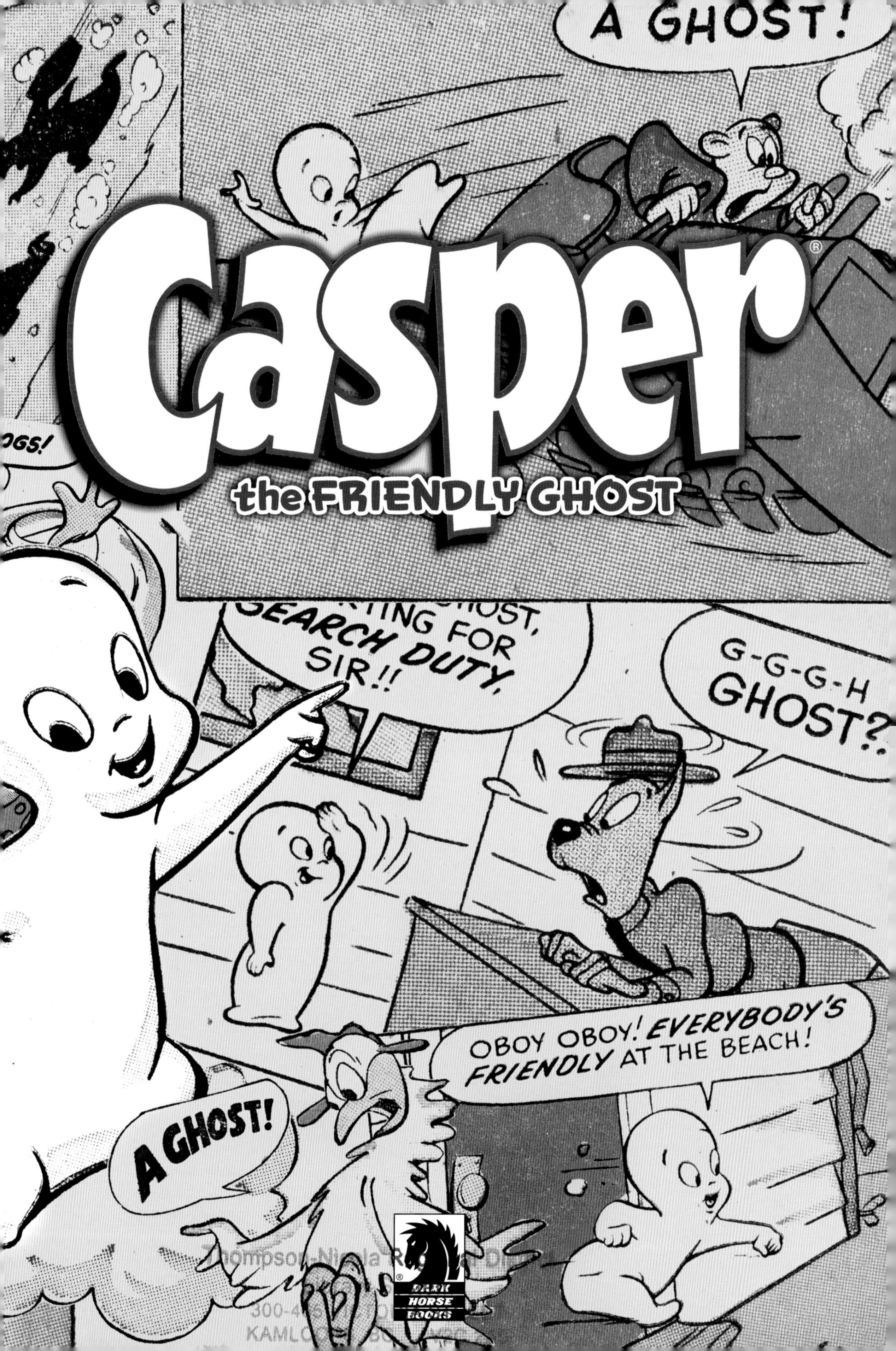
A GHOST!
SEARCH DUTY, SIR!!
G-G-G-H GHOST?
OBOY OBOY! EVERYBODY'S FRIENDLY AT THE BEACH!
A GHOST!
DARK HORSE BOOKS

Casper
the FRIENDLY GHOST

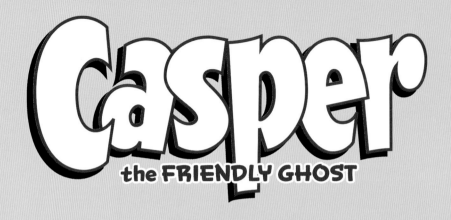

Publisher: **Mike Richardson**
Editorial Director: **Davey Estrada**
Editor: **Shawna Gore**
Book design and compilation: **Leslie Cabarga**

This book collects
Casper the Friendly Ghost
issue #1, September 1949,
published by Jubilee Publications, Inc.,
and
Harvey Comics Hits
issue #61 (also listed as
Casper the Friendly Ghost *issue #6),*
October 1952, published by
Harvey Publications, Inc.

First edition: November 2009
1 3 5 7 9 10 8 6 4 2
ISBN 978-1-59582-467-7

Published by Dark Horse Books, a division of Dark Horse Comics, Inc., 10956 SE Main Street, Milwaukie, Oregon 97222.

darkhorse.com

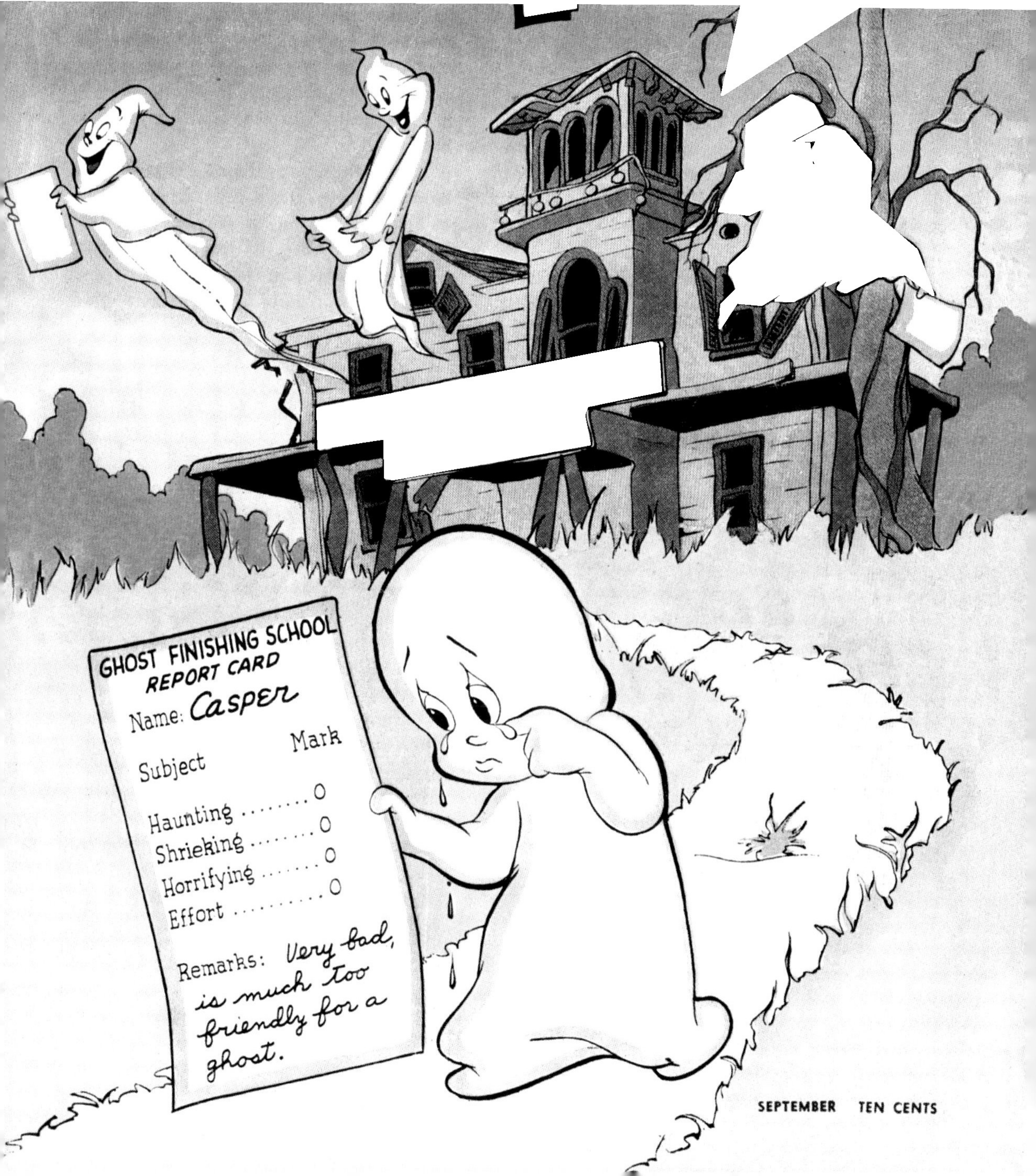

GHOST FINISHING SCHOOL
REPORT CARD
Name: Casper
Subject
Mark
Haunting 0
Shrieking 0
Horrifying 0
Effort 0
Remarks: Very bad, is much too friendly for a ghost.
SEPTEMBER TEN CENTS

CREEPY TOWN TERROR

By Oliver Towne

NOBODY PAID MUCH attention when Sam Centipede shuffled down Main Street. Watching him walk made most everyone dizzy because no one had ever been able to figure out how Sam knew which foot to raise and which one to lower without tripping himself.

But Sam's undulating underpinnings shivered to a halt outside the window of Crick Crickett's cobbler shop. Scratching his head with a down turned feeler, Sam gazed at the fine assortment of shoes in the window. The fish scale oxfords caught his fancy, and he shuffled through the door.

Crick Crickett almost swallowed a mouthful of boot nails when he turned from his work bench and saw who had stepped in. "You!" he chirped. "A shoemaker's dream come true! But all kidding aside, Sam, with one hundred feet wouldn't it be wiser to continue going barefooted? Fifty pairs of shoes will cost you a stack of bills."

"Don't make me change my mind," Sam wheezed. "I've been saving my coins and folding money for the great day. Measure my tootsies and make up a hundred fish scale oxfords to fit them. After my feet are shod, I'll start saving again for a rainy day. One hundred rubbers will cost me plenty, too."

"No snap indeed," chirped Crick as he stepped around the bench with a foot measure. "After buying shoes, you'll really have to stretch your budget to buy rubbers."

Crick patiently measured each one of Sam's many feet, and found them to be exactly the same size. "You want them with buckles, of course," Crick chirped. "It would take all day for you to tie laces. They will be ready in about three weeks, my friend. Perfect fit guaranteed or your money will be cheerfully refunded."

"It's a deal," wheezed Sam, rubbing his feelers together briskly. "Cash on the line before I walk out with them."

As Sam shuffled out of the cobbler's shop, he failed to notice the notorious bug thug, Deedee Tee lurking behind a stack of leaf leather. Deedee Tee grinned evilly while he watched the centipede ramble down the street for he had overheard Sam's conversation with the cobbler.

That night Creepy Town was awakened by a blood curdling scream. Sheriff Tick sprang out of bed, slapped on his gun belt, ran from his walnut shell house and leaped to the saddle of his trusty June bug, Jasper. The hard-shelled critter snorted, shook the dew from his wings and whizzed off over the rooftops.

"That scream came from the edge of town," the sheriff snarled. "Ah, yes — look! I see a light on Sam Centipede's porch. Get over there fast, Jasper!"

But even as Sheriff Tick dashed across Sam's porch he could see through the open door that he was too late to help the hundred-legged citizen. Sam lay still in the middle of the room. In his back was a rose thorn. He had been stabbed to death. Murdered by some fiendish prowler.

Buck, Benny and Bob Beetle pressed through the narrow door as a crowd gathered in the street outside. "Anything we can do, Sheriff?" Bob asked.

"Right!" snapped the sheriff. "One of you run and call the coroner. "Benny — you stand guard by the door and let no one inside. A crime has been committed, and I've got to search for a clue and a motive."

The sheriff turned to his task with grim determination and his efforts were soon rewarded. Under the kitchen sink he found an empty cash

(Continued On Inside Back Cover)

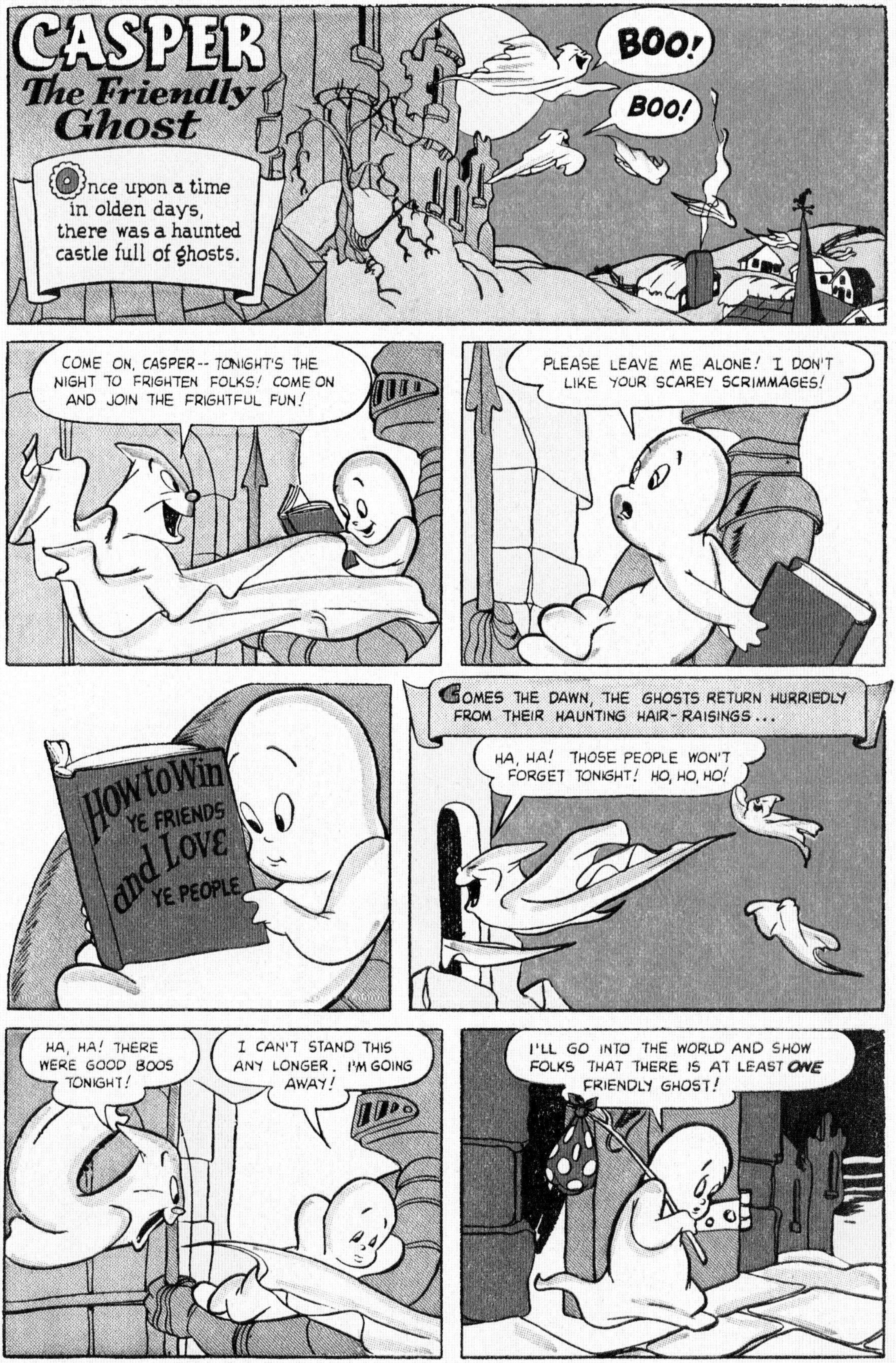
CASPER
The Friendly Ghost
Once upon a time in olden days, there was a haunted castle full of ghosts.
BOO!
BOO!
COME ON, CASPER-- TONIGHT'S THE NIGHT TO FRIGHTEN FOLKS! COME ON AND JOIN THE FRIGHTFUL FUN!
PLEASE LEAVE ME ALONE! I DON'T LIKE YOUR SCAREY SCRIMMAGES!
HOW to WIN YE FRIENDS and LOVE YE PEOPLE
COMES THE DAWN, THE GHOSTS RETURN HURRIEDLY FROM THEIR HAUNTING HAIR-RAISINGS...
HA, HA! THOSE PEOPLE WON'T FORGET TONIGHT! HO, HO, HO!
HA, HA! THERE WERE GOOD BOOS TONIGHT!
I CAN'T STAND THIS ANY LONGER. I'M GOING AWAY!
I'LL GO INTO THE WORLD AND SHOW FOLKS THAT THERE IS AT LEAST ONE FRIENDLY GHOST!

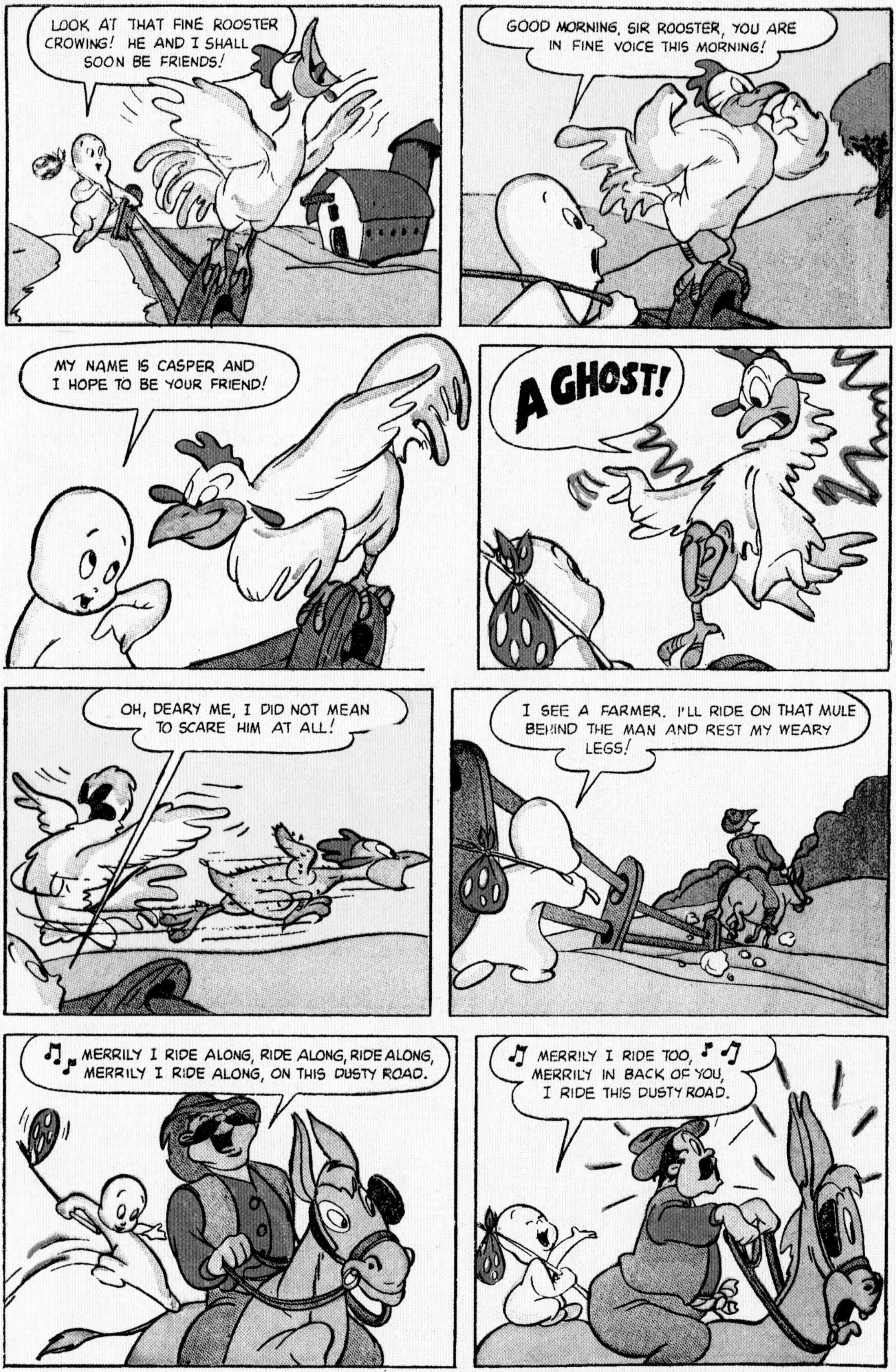
LOOK AT THAT FINE ROOSTER CROWING! HE AND I SHALL SOON BE FRIENDS!
GOOD MORNING, SIR ROOSTER, YOU ARE IN FINE VOICE THIS MORNING!
MY NAME IS CASPER AND I HOPE TO BE YOUR FRIEND!
A GHOST!
OH, DEARY ME, I DID NOT MEAN TO SCARE HIM AT ALL!
I SEE A FARMER. I'LL RIDE ON THAT MULE BEHIND THE MAN AND REST MY WEARY LEGS!
MERRILY I RIDE ALONG, RIDE ALONG, RIDE ALONG, MERRILY I RIDE ALONG, ON THIS DUSTY ROAD.
MERRILY I RIDE TOO, MERRILY IN BACK OF YOU, I RIDE THIS DUSTY ROAD.

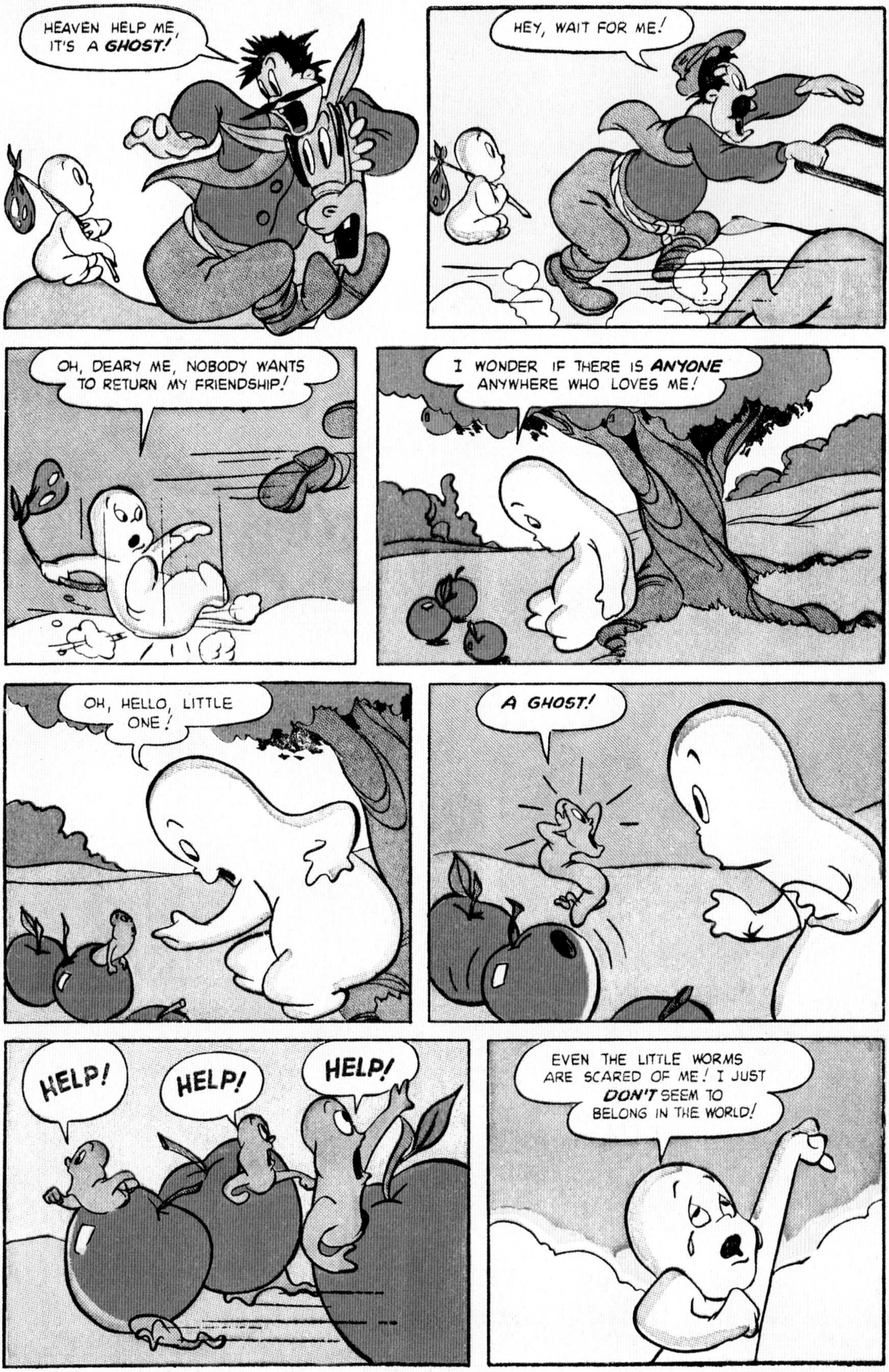
HEAVEN HELP ME, IT'S A GHOST!
HEY, WAIT FOR ME!
OH, DEARY ME, NOBODY WANTS TO RETURN MY FRIENDSHIP!
I WONDER IF THERE IS ANYONE ANYWHERE WHO LOVES ME!
OH, HELLO, LITTLE ONE!
A GHOST!
HELP!
HELP!
HELP!
EVEN THE LITTLE WORMS ARE SCARED OF ME! I JUST DON'T SEEM TO BELONG IN THE WORLD!

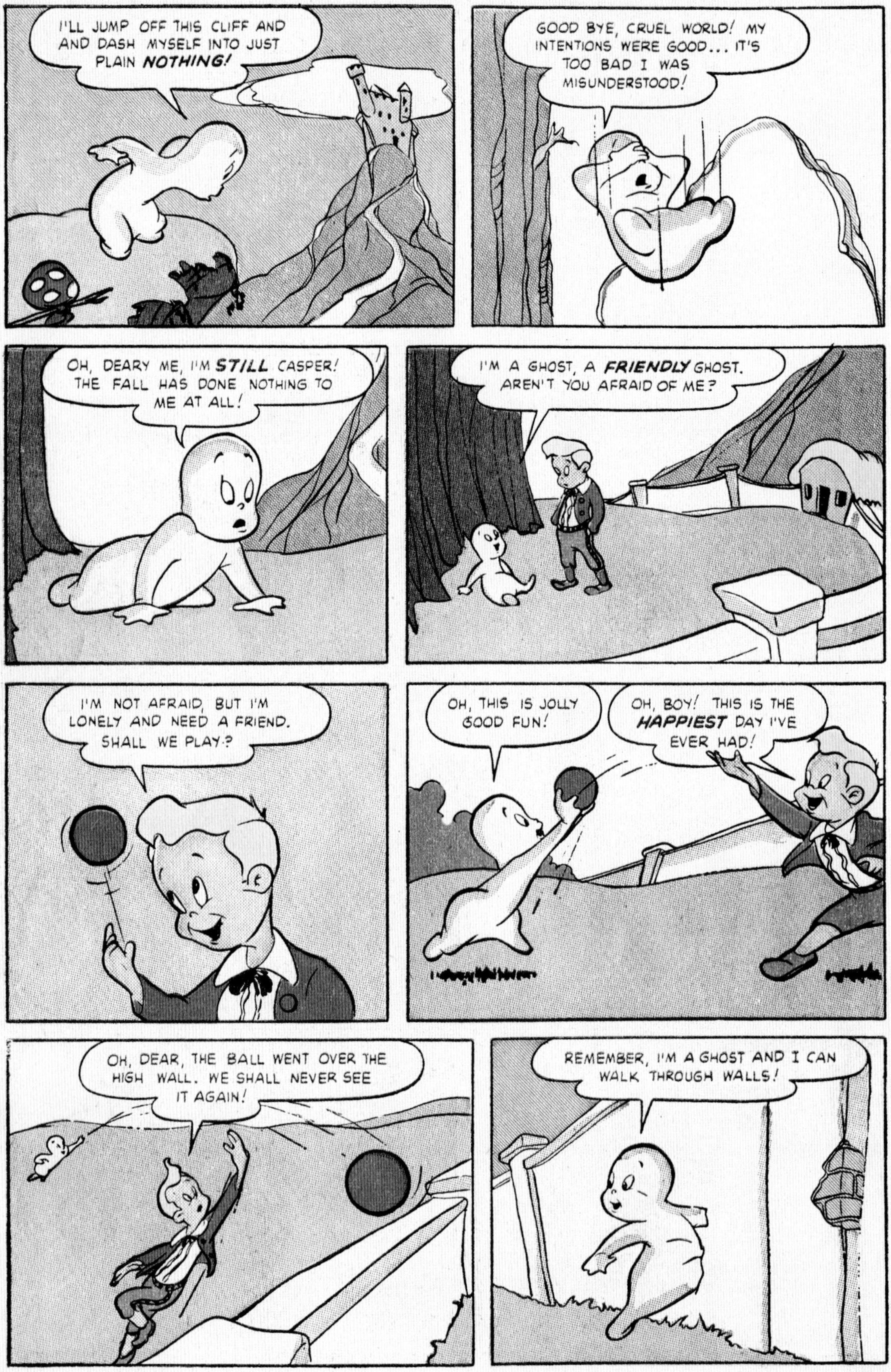
I'LL JUMP OFF THIS CLIFF AND AND DASH MYSELF INTO JUST PLAIN **NOTHING!**
GOOD BYE, CRUEL WORLD! MY INTENTIONS WERE GOOD... IT'S TOO BAD I WAS MISUNDERSTOOD!
OH, DEARY ME, I'M **STILL** CASPER! THE FALL HAS DONE NOTHING TO ME AT ALL!
I'M A GHOST, A **FRIENDLY** GHOST. AREN'T YOU AFRAID OF ME?
I'M NOT AFRAID, BUT I'M LONELY AND NEED A FRIEND. SHALL WE PLAY?
OH, THIS IS JOLLY GOOD FUN!
OH, BOY! THIS IS THE **HAPPIEST** DAY I'VE EVER HAD!
OH, DEAR, THE BALL WENT OVER THE HIGH WALL. WE SHALL NEVER SEE IT AGAIN!
REMEMBER, I'M A GHOST AND I CAN WALK THROUGH WALLS!

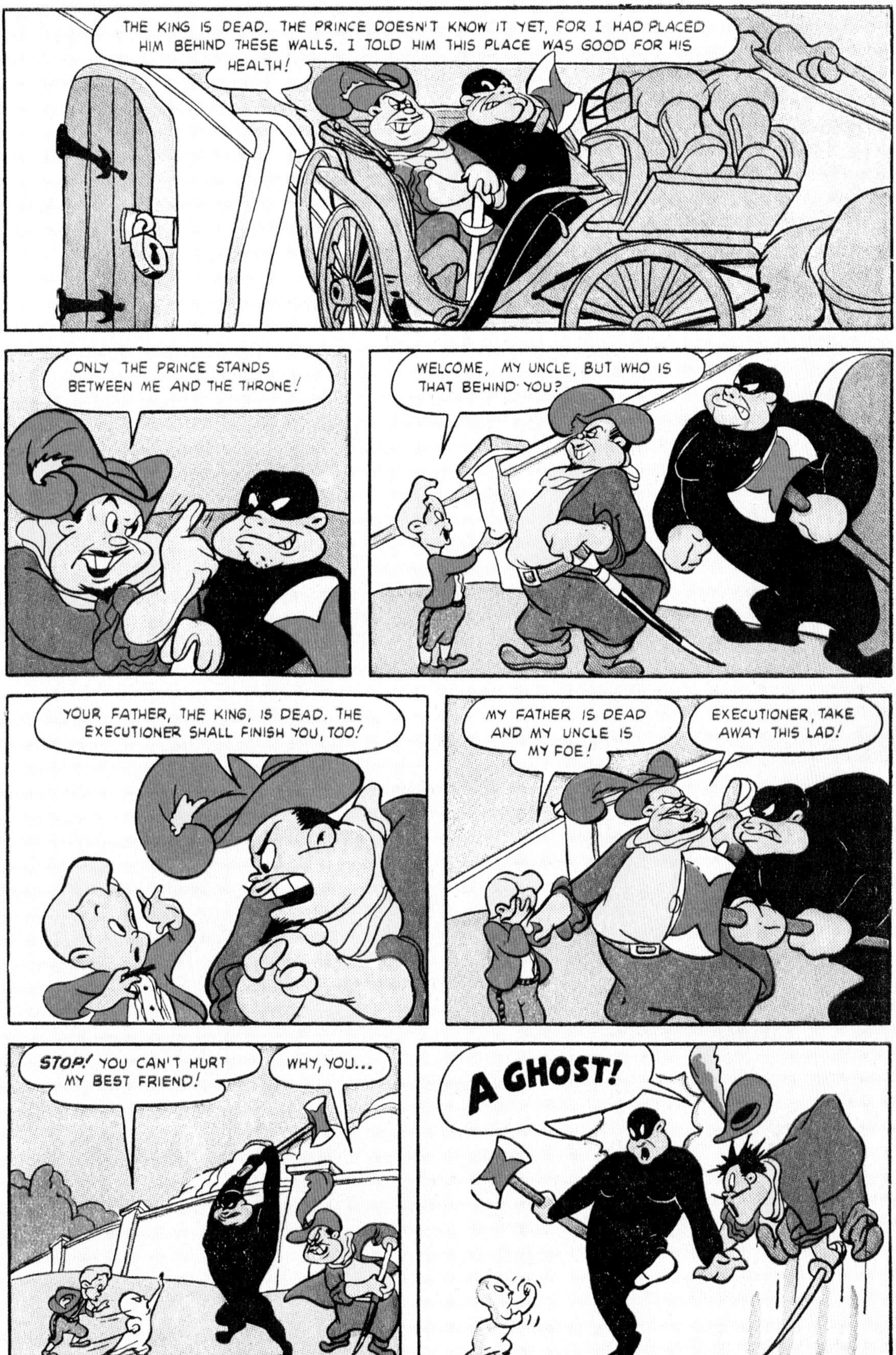
THE KING IS DEAD. THE PRINCE DOESN'T KNOW IT YET, FOR I HAD PLACED HIM BEHIND THESE WALLS. I TOLD HIM THIS PLACE WAS GOOD FOR HIS HEALTH!
ONLY THE PRINCE STANDS BETWEEN ME AND THE THRONE!
WELCOME, MY UNCLE, BUT WHO IS THAT BEHIND YOU?
YOUR FATHER, THE KING, IS DEAD. THE EXECUTIONER SHALL FINISH YOU, TOO!
MY FATHER IS DEAD AND MY UNCLE IS MY FOE!
EXECUTIONER, TAKE AWAY THIS LAD!
STOP! YOU CAN'T HURT MY BEST FRIEND!
WHY, YOU...
A GHOST!

HELP! HELP!! A GHOST! A REAL LIVE GHOST!
HOW CAN I THANK YOU, CASPER, FOR SAVING MY LIFE AND MY THRONE?
JUST LET ME ALWAYS BE YOUR FRIEND!
LONG LIVE THE KING!
HIP, HIP, HOORAY FOR CASPER!
The End

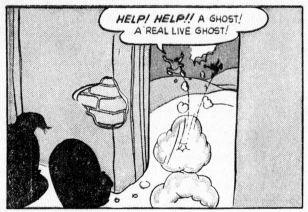

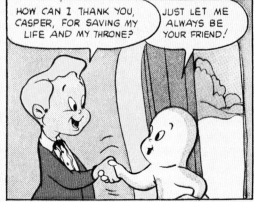

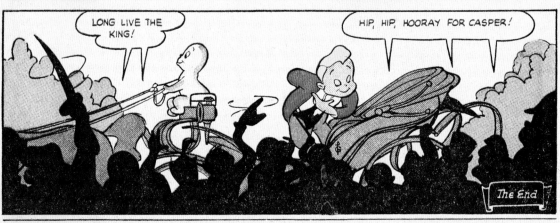

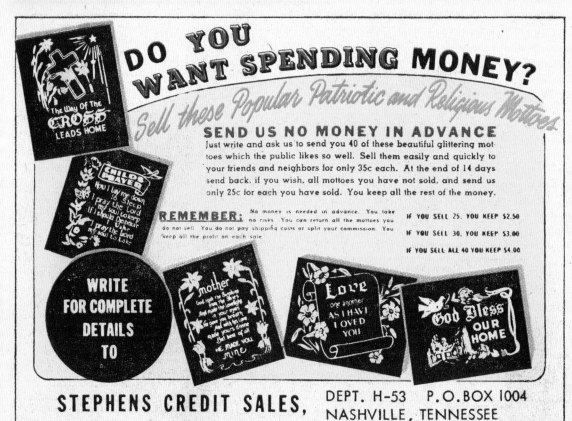

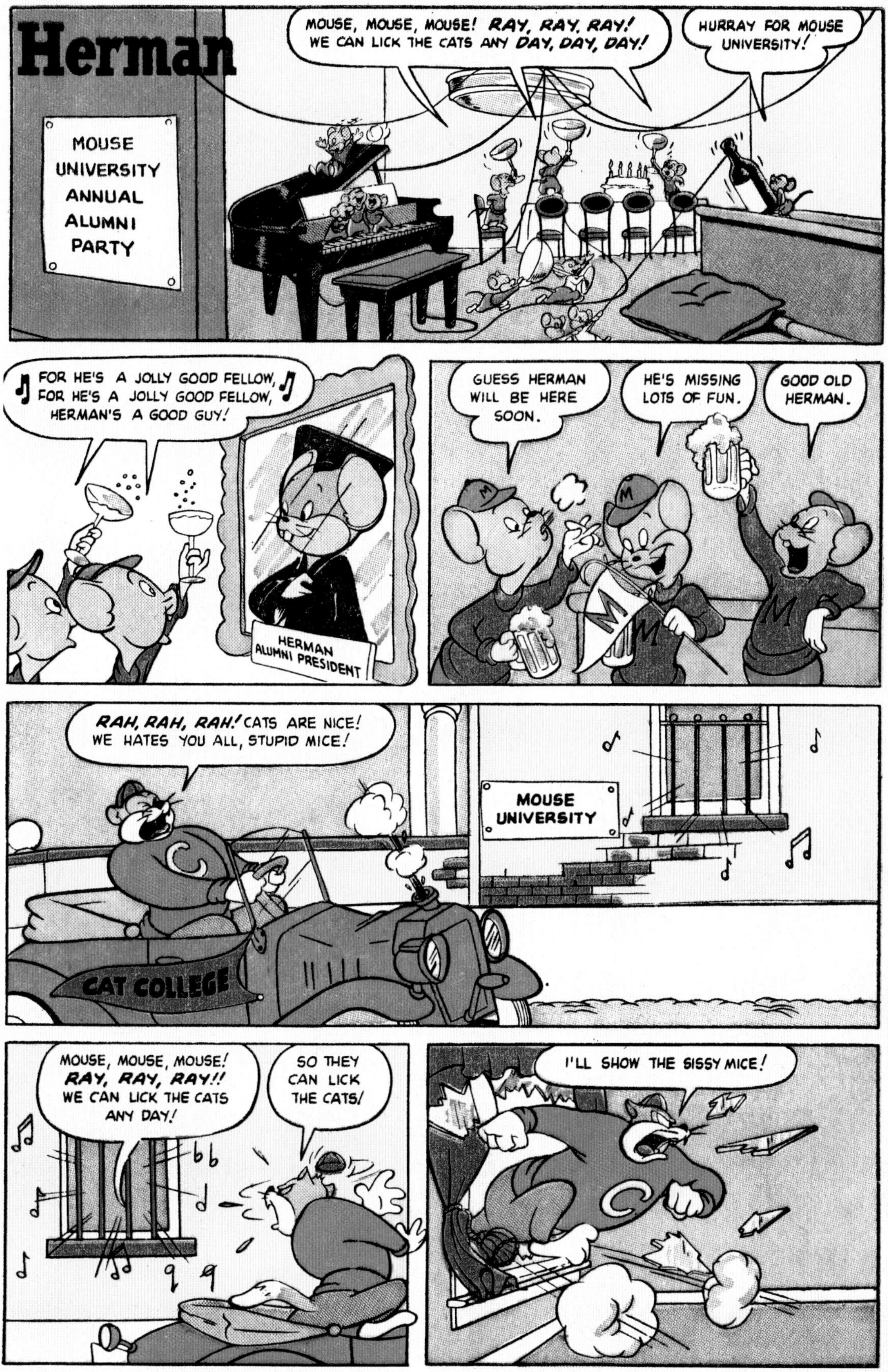
Herman
MOUSE, MOUSE, MOUSE! RAY, RAY, RAY! WE CAN LICK THE CATS ANY DAY, DAY, DAY!
HURRAY FOR MOUSE UNIVERSITY!
MOUSE UNIVERSITY ANNUAL ALUMNI PARTY
FOR HE'S A JOLLY GOOD FELLOW, FOR HE'S A JOLLY GOOD FELLOW, HERMAN'S A GOOD GUY!
HERMAN ALUMNI PRESIDENT
GUESS HERMAN WILL BE HERE SOON.
HE'S MISSING LOTS OF FUN.
GOOD OLD HERMAN.
RAH, RAH, RAH! CATS ARE NICE! WE HATES YOU ALL, STUPID MICE!
MOUSE UNIVERSITY
CAT COLLEGE
MOUSE, MOUSE, MOUSE! RAY, RAY, RAY!! WE CAN LICK THE CATS ANY DAY!
SO THEY CAN LICK THE CATS!
I'LL SHOW THE SISSY MICE!

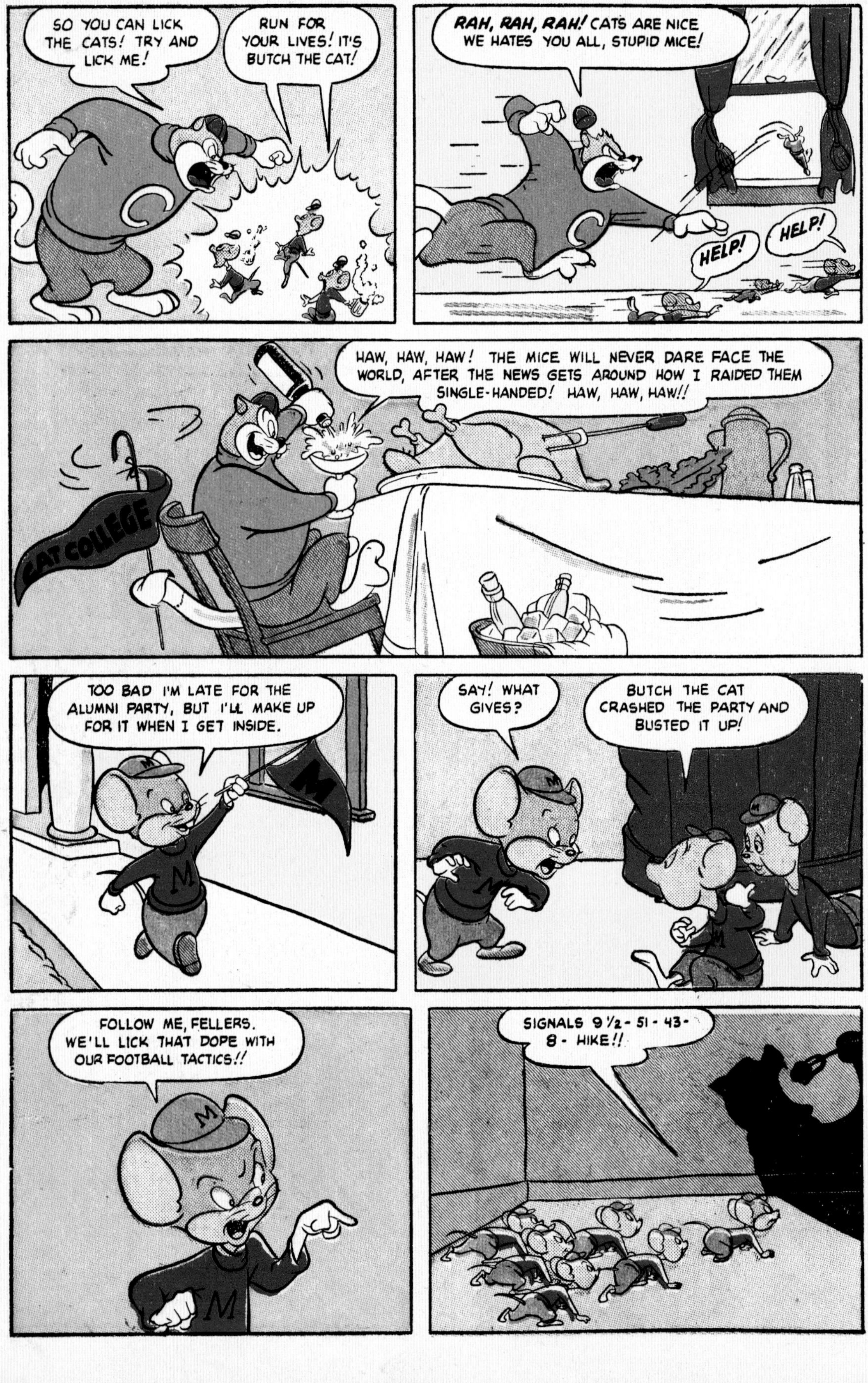
SO YOU CAN LICK THE CATS! TRY AND LICK ME!
RUN FOR YOUR LIVES! IT'S BUTCH THE CAT!
RAH, RAH, RAH! CATS ARE NICE WE HATES YOU ALL, STUPID MICE!
HELP!
HELP!
HAW, HAW, HAW! THE MICE WILL NEVER DARE FACE THE WORLD, AFTER THE NEWS GETS AROUND HOW I RAIDED THEM SINGLE-HANDED! HAW, HAW, HAW!!
CAT COLLEGE
TOO BAD I'M LATE FOR THE ALUMNI PARTY, BUT I'LL MAKE UP FOR IT WHEN I GET INSIDE.
SAY! WHAT GIVES?
BUTCH THE CAT CRASHED THE PARTY AND BUSTED IT UP!
FOLLOW ME, FELLERS. WE'LL LICK THAT DOPE WITH OUR FOOTBALL TACTICS!!
SIGNALS 9 1/2 - 51 - 43 - 8 - HIKE!!

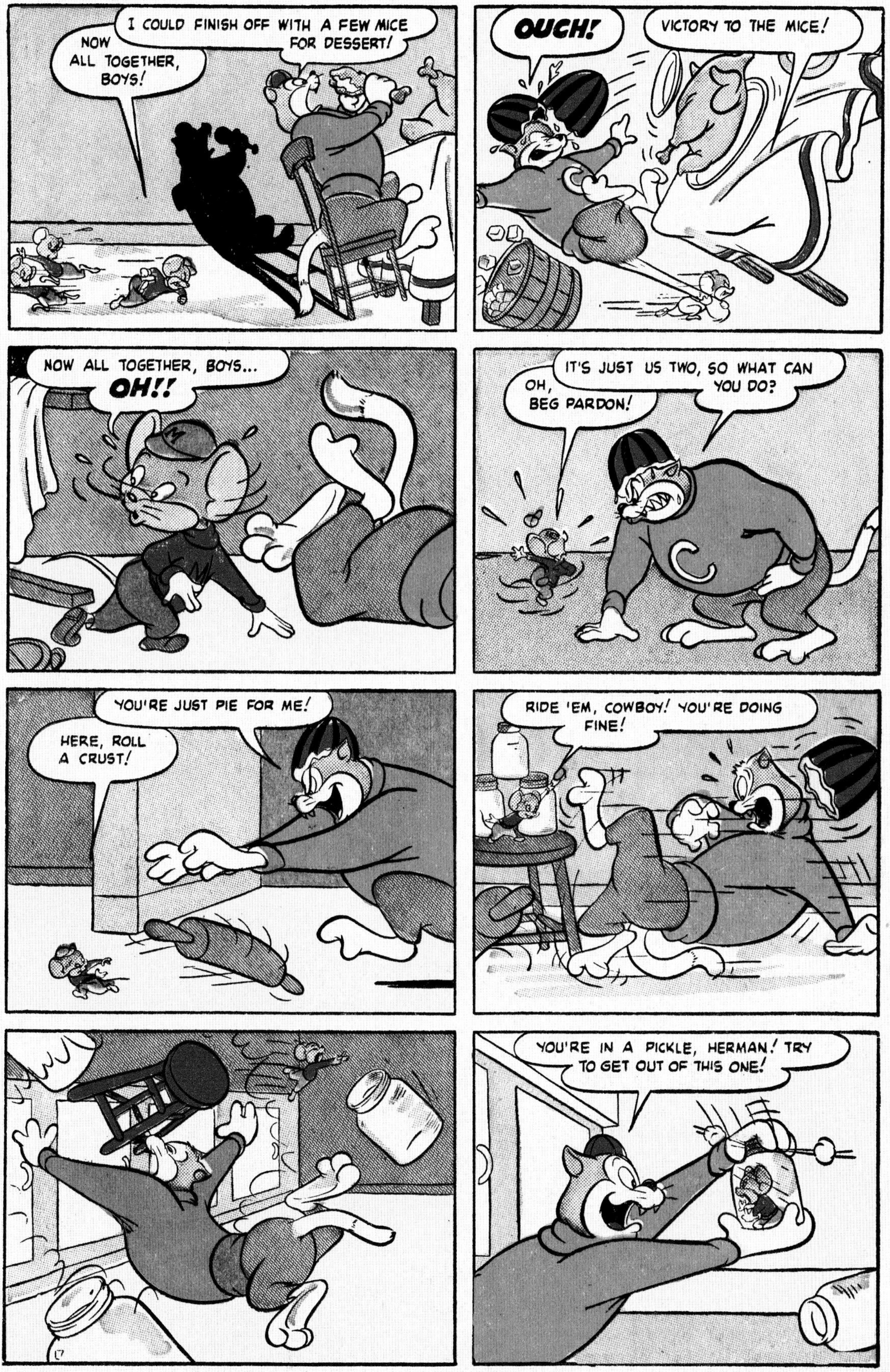
I COULD FINISH OFF WITH A FEW MICE FOR DESSERT!
NOW ALL TOGETHER, BOYS!
OUCH!
VICTORY TO THE MICE!
NOW ALL TOGETHER, BOYS... OH!!
OH, BEG PARDON!
IT'S JUST US TWO, SO WHAT CAN YOU DO?
YOU'RE JUST PIE FOR ME!
HERE, ROLL A CRUST!
RIDE 'EM, COWBOY! YOU'RE DOING FINE!
YOU'RE IN A PICKLE, HERMAN! TRY TO GET OUT OF THIS ONE!
17

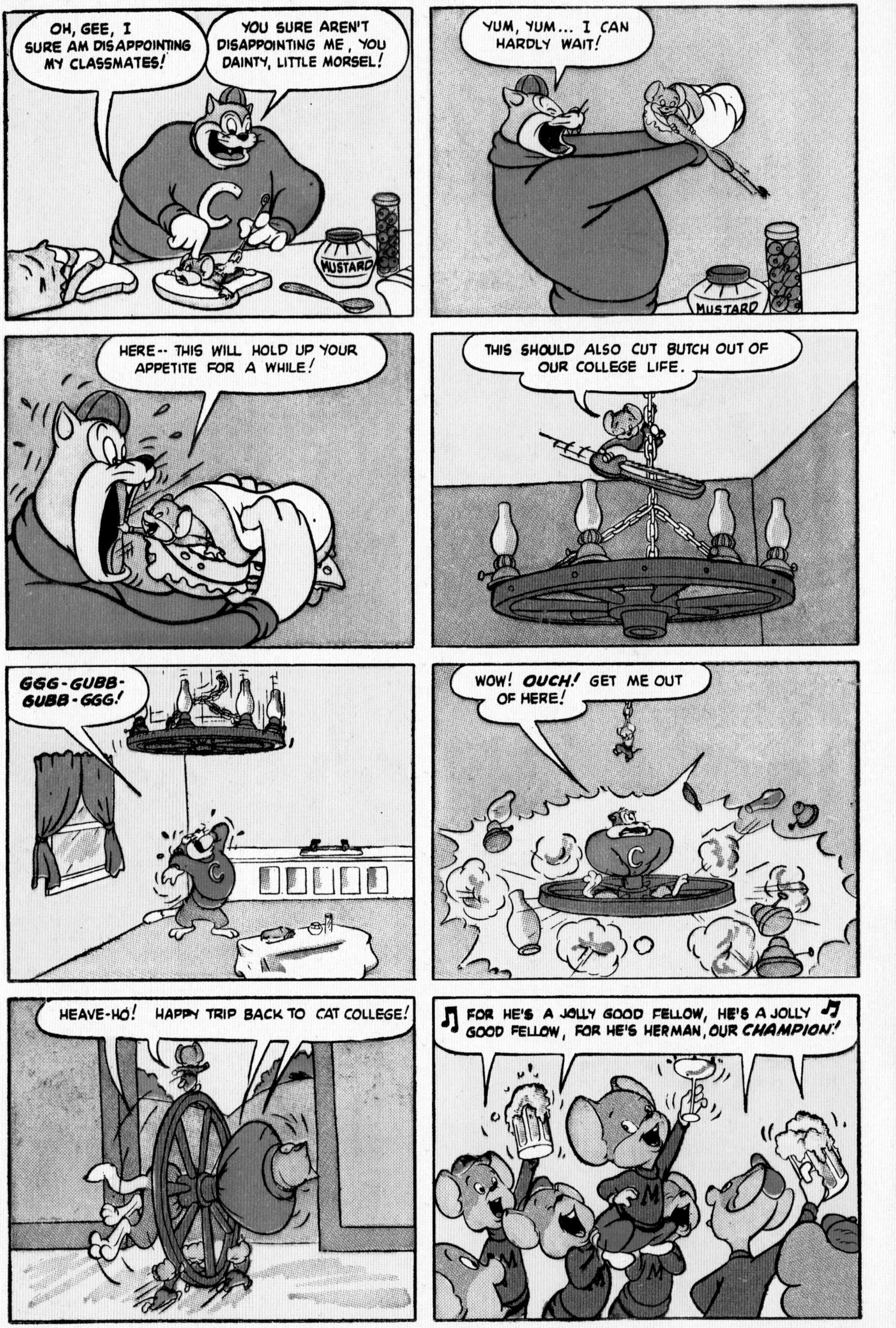
OH, GEE, I SURE AM DISAPPOINTING MY CLASSMATES!
YOU SURE AREN'T DISAPPOINTING ME, YOU DAINTY, LITTLE MORSEL!
MUSTARD
YUM, YUM... I CAN HARDLY WAIT!
MUSTARD
HERE-- THIS WILL HOLD UP YOUR APPETITE FOR A WHILE!
THIS SHOULD ALSO CUT BUTCH OUT OF OUR COLLEGE LIFE.
GGG-GUBB-GUBB-GGG!
WOW! OUCH! GET ME OUT OF HERE!
HEAVE-HO! HAPPY TRIP BACK TO CAT COLLEGE!
♫ FOR HE'S A JOLLY GOOD FELLOW, HE'S A JOLLY ♫ GOOD FELLOW, FOR HE'S HERMAN, OUR CHAMPION!

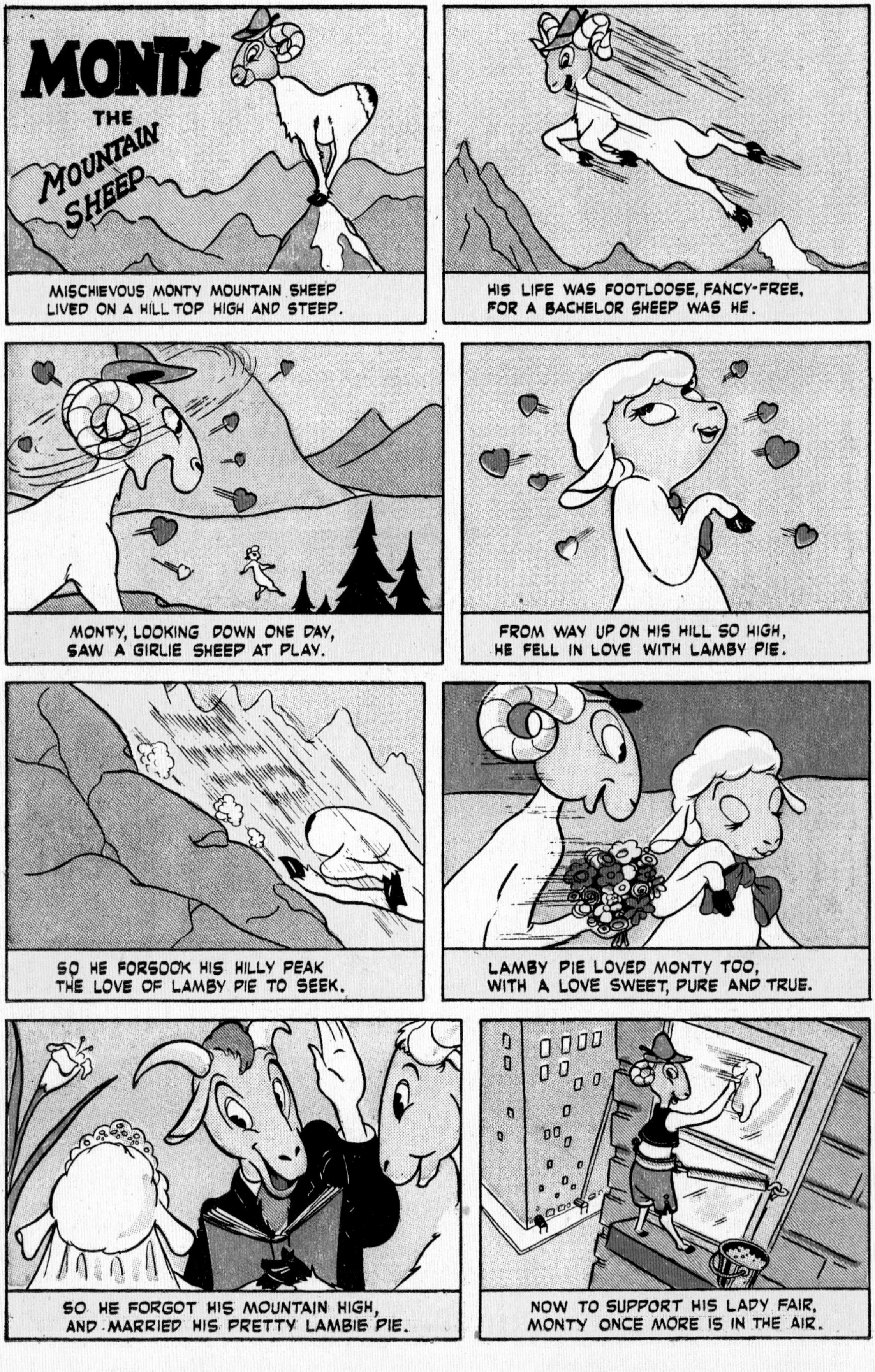
MONTY THE MOUNTAIN SHEEP
MISCHIEVOUS MONTY MOUNTAIN SHEEP LIVED ON A HILL TOP HIGH AND STEEP.
HIS LIFE WAS FOOTLOOSE, FANCY-FREE, FOR A BACHELOR SHEEP WAS HE.
MONTY, LOOKING DOWN ONE DAY, SAW A GIRLIE SHEEP AT PLAY.
FROM WAY UP ON HIS HILL SO HIGH, HE FELL IN LOVE WITH LAMBY PIE.
SO HE FORSOOK HIS HILLY PEAK THE LOVE OF LAMBY PIE TO SEEK.
LAMBY PIE LOVED MONTY TOO, WITH A LOVE SWEET, PURE AND TRUE.
SO HE FORGOT HIS MOUNTAIN HIGH, AND MARRIED HIS PRETTY LAMBIE PIE.
NOW TO SUPPORT HIS LADY FAIR, MONTY ONCE MORE IS IN THE AIR.

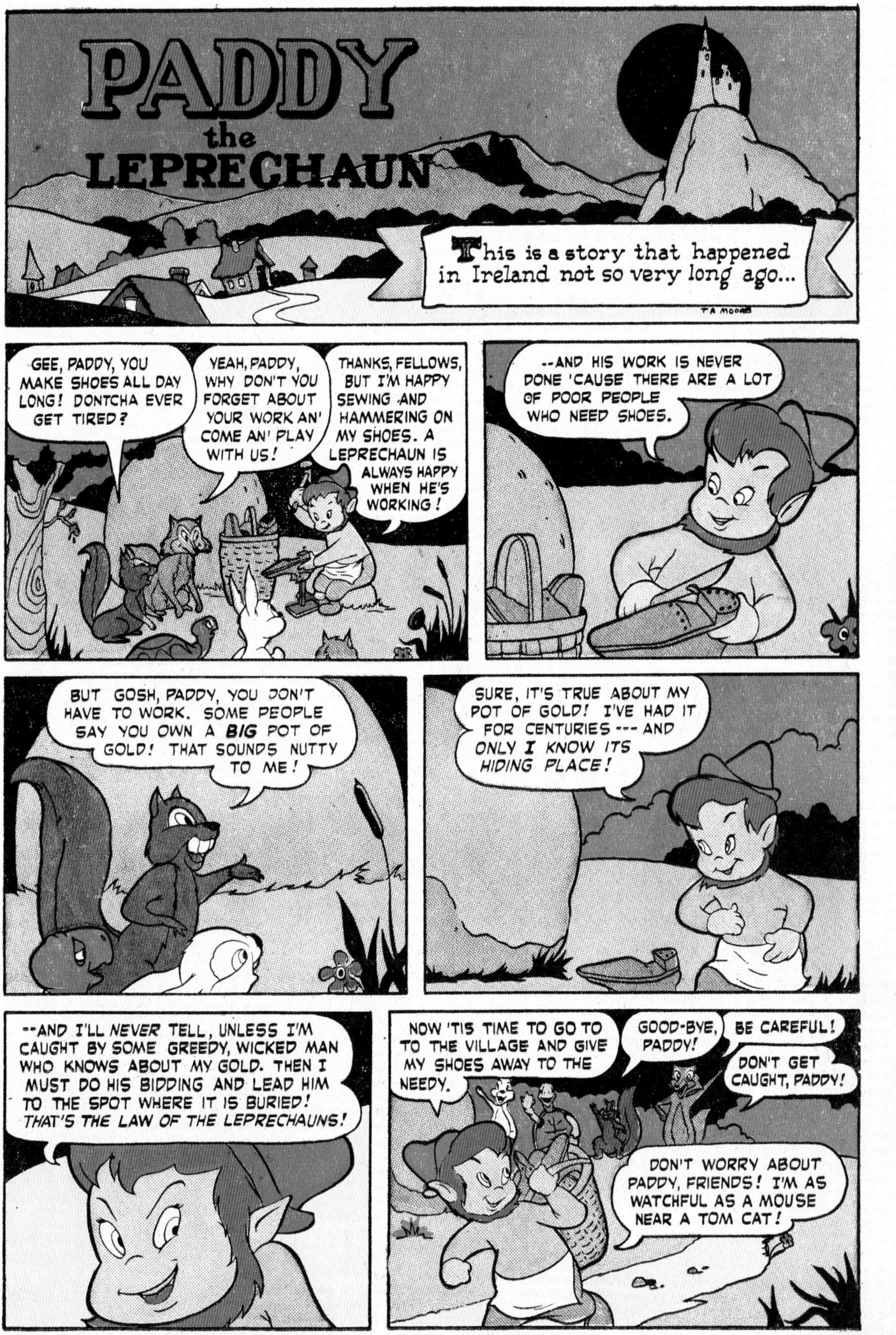
PADDY
the
LEPRECHAUN
This is a story that happened in Ireland not so very long ago...
T.A. MOORE
GEE, PADDY, YOU MAKE SHOES ALL DAY LONG! DONTCHA EVER GET TIRED?
YEAH, PADDY, WHY DON'T YOU FORGET ABOUT YOUR WORK AN' COME AN' PLAY WITH US!
THANKS, FELLOWS, BUT I'M HAPPY SEWING AND HAMMERING ON MY SHOES. A LEPRECHAUN IS ALWAYS HAPPY WHEN HE'S WORKING!
--AND HIS WORK IS NEVER DONE 'CAUSE THERE ARE A LOT OF POOR PEOPLE WHO NEED SHOES.
BUT GOSH, PADDY, YOU DON'T HAVE TO WORK. SOME PEOPLE SAY YOU OWN A BIG POT OF GOLD! THAT SOUNDS NUTTY TO ME!
SURE, IT'S TRUE ABOUT MY POT OF GOLD! I'VE HAD IT FOR CENTURIES --- AND ONLY I KNOW ITS HIDING PLACE!
--AND I'LL NEVER TELL, UNLESS I'M CAUGHT BY SOME GREEDY, WICKED MAN WHO KNOWS ABOUT MY GOLD. THEN I MUST DO HIS BIDDING AND LEAD HIM TO THE SPOT WHERE IT IS BURIED! THAT'S THE LAW OF THE LEPRECHAUNS!
NOW 'TIS TIME TO GO TO TO THE VILLAGE AND GIVE MY SHOES AWAY TO THE NEEDY.
GOOD-BYE, PADDY!
BE CAREFUL!
DON'T GET CAUGHT, PADDY!
DON'T WORRY ABOUT PADDY, FRIENDS! I'M AS WATCHFUL AS A MOUSE NEAR A TOM CAT!

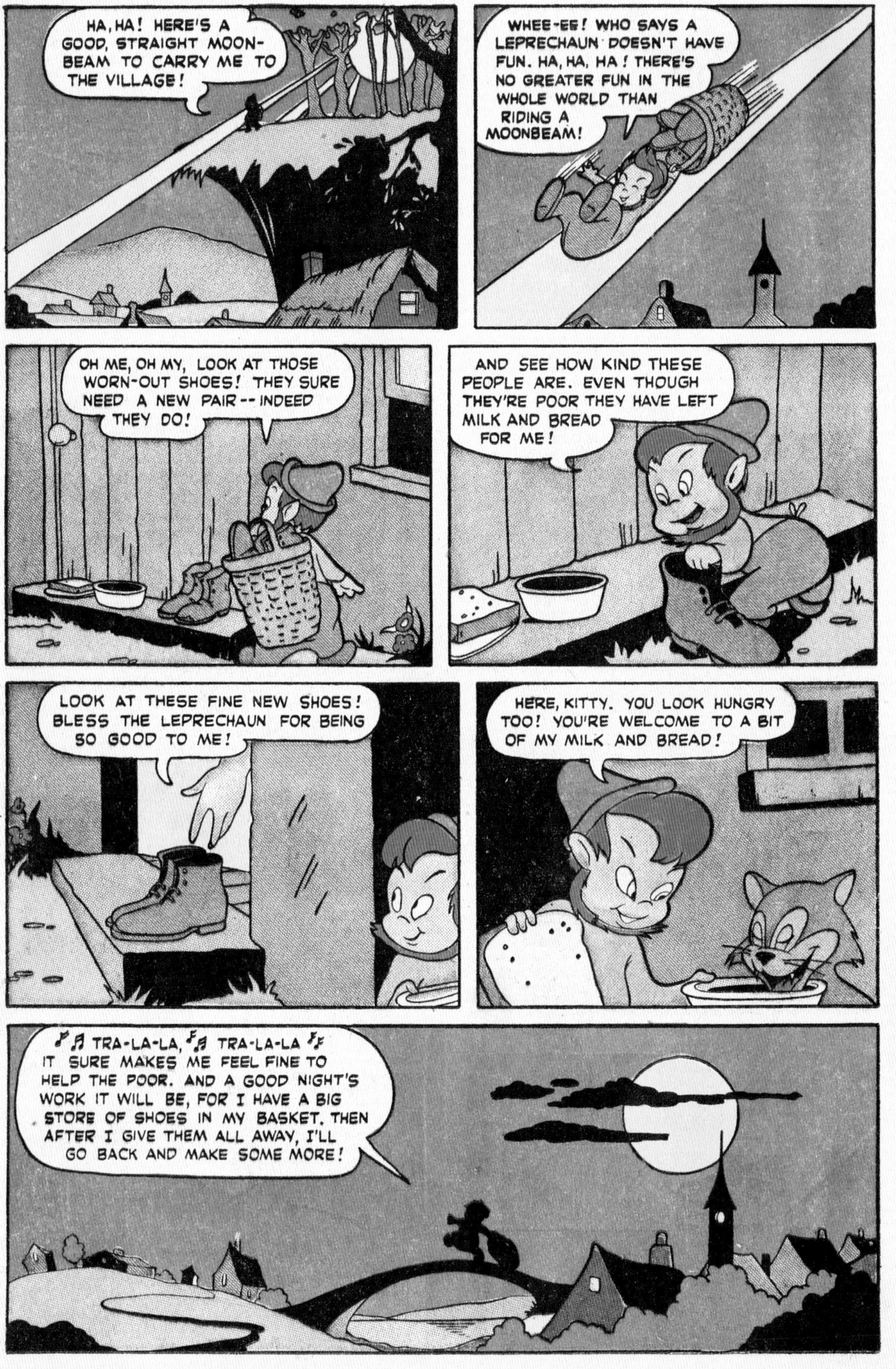

HA, HA! HERE'S A GOOD, STRAIGHT MOON-BEAM TO CARRY ME TO THE VILLAGE!
WHEE-EE! WHO SAYS A LEPRECHAUN DOESN'T HAVE FUN. HA, HA, HA! THERE'S NO GREATER FUN IN THE WHOLE WORLD THAN RIDING A MOONBEAM!
OH ME, OH MY, LOOK AT THOSE WORN-OUT SHOES! THEY SURE NEED A NEW PAIR -- INDEED THEY DO!
AND SEE HOW KIND THESE PEOPLE ARE. EVEN THOUGH THEY'RE POOR THEY HAVE LEFT MILK AND BREAD FOR ME!
LOOK AT THESE FINE NEW SHOES! BLESS THE LEPRECHAUN FOR BEING SO GOOD TO ME!
HERE, KITTY. YOU LOOK HUNGRY TOO! YOU'RE WELCOME TO A BIT OF MY MILK AND BREAD!
TRA-LA-LA, TRA-LA-LA IT SURE MAKES ME FEEL FINE TO HELP THE POOR. AND A GOOD NIGHT'S WORK IT WILL BE, FOR I HAVE A BIG STORE OF SHOES IN MY BASKET. THEN AFTER I GIVE THEM ALL AWAY, I'LL GO BACK AND MAKE SOME MORE!

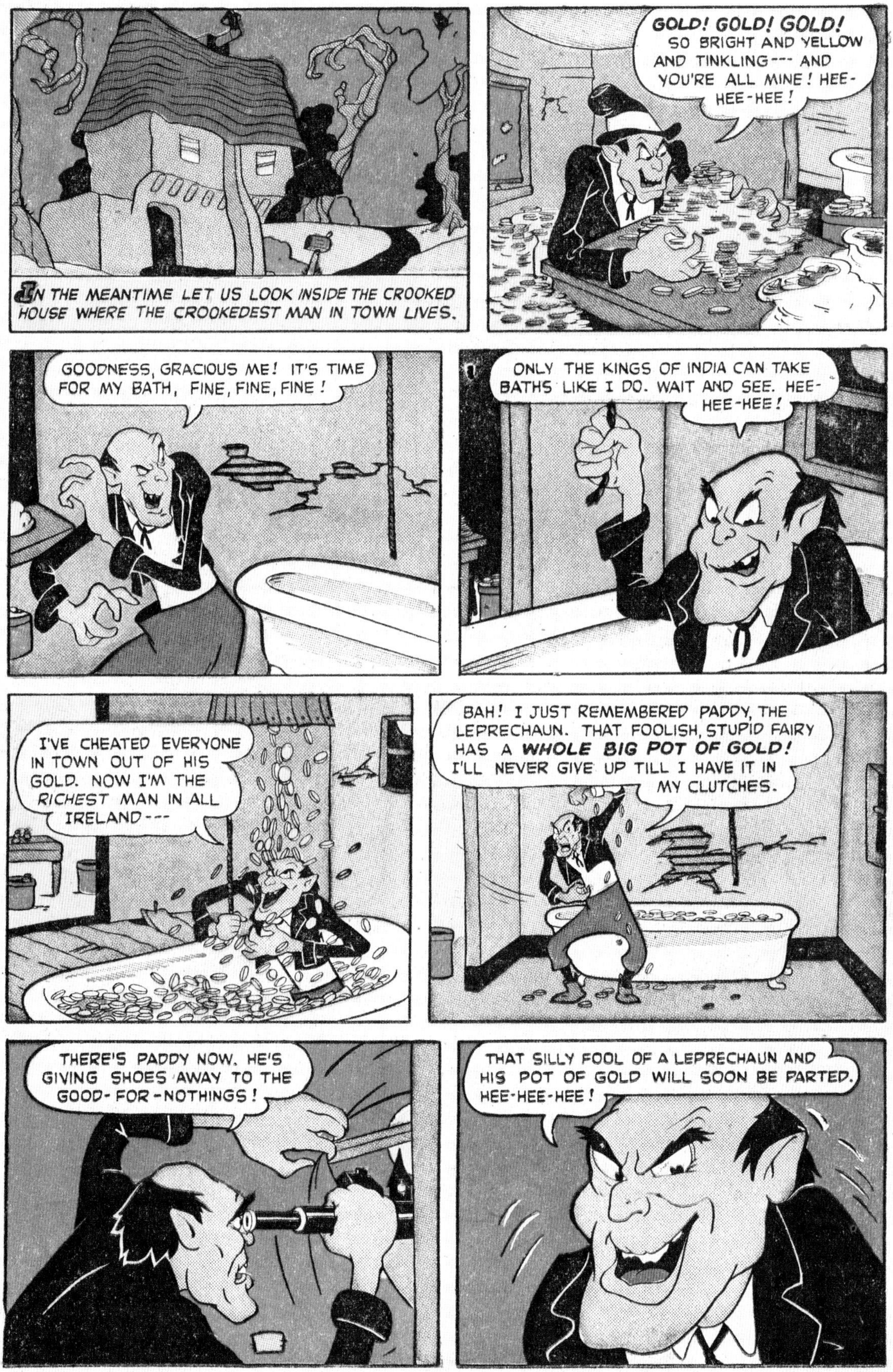
IN THE MEANTIME LET US LOOK INSIDE THE CROOKED HOUSE WHERE THE CROOKEDEST MAN IN TOWN LIVES.
GOLD! GOLD! GOLD! SO BRIGHT AND YELLOW AND TINKLING--- AND YOU'RE ALL MINE! HEE-HEE-HEE!
GOODNESS, GRACIOUS ME! IT'S TIME FOR MY BATH, FINE, FINE, FINE!
ONLY THE KINGS OF INDIA CAN TAKE BATHS LIKE I DO. WAIT AND SEE. HEE-HEE-HEE!
I'VE CHEATED EVERYONE IN TOWN OUT OF HIS GOLD. NOW I'M THE RICHEST MAN IN ALL IRELAND---
BAH! I JUST REMEMBERED PADDY, THE LEPRECHAUN. THAT FOOLISH, STUPID FAIRY HAS A WHOLE BIG POT OF GOLD! I'LL NEVER GIVE UP TILL I HAVE IT IN MY CLUTCHES.
THERE'S PADDY NOW. HE'S GIVING SHOES AWAY TO THE GOOD-FOR-NOTHINGS!
THAT SILLY FOOL OF A LEPRECHAUN AND HIS POT OF GOLD WILL SOON BE PARTED. HEE-HEE-HEE!

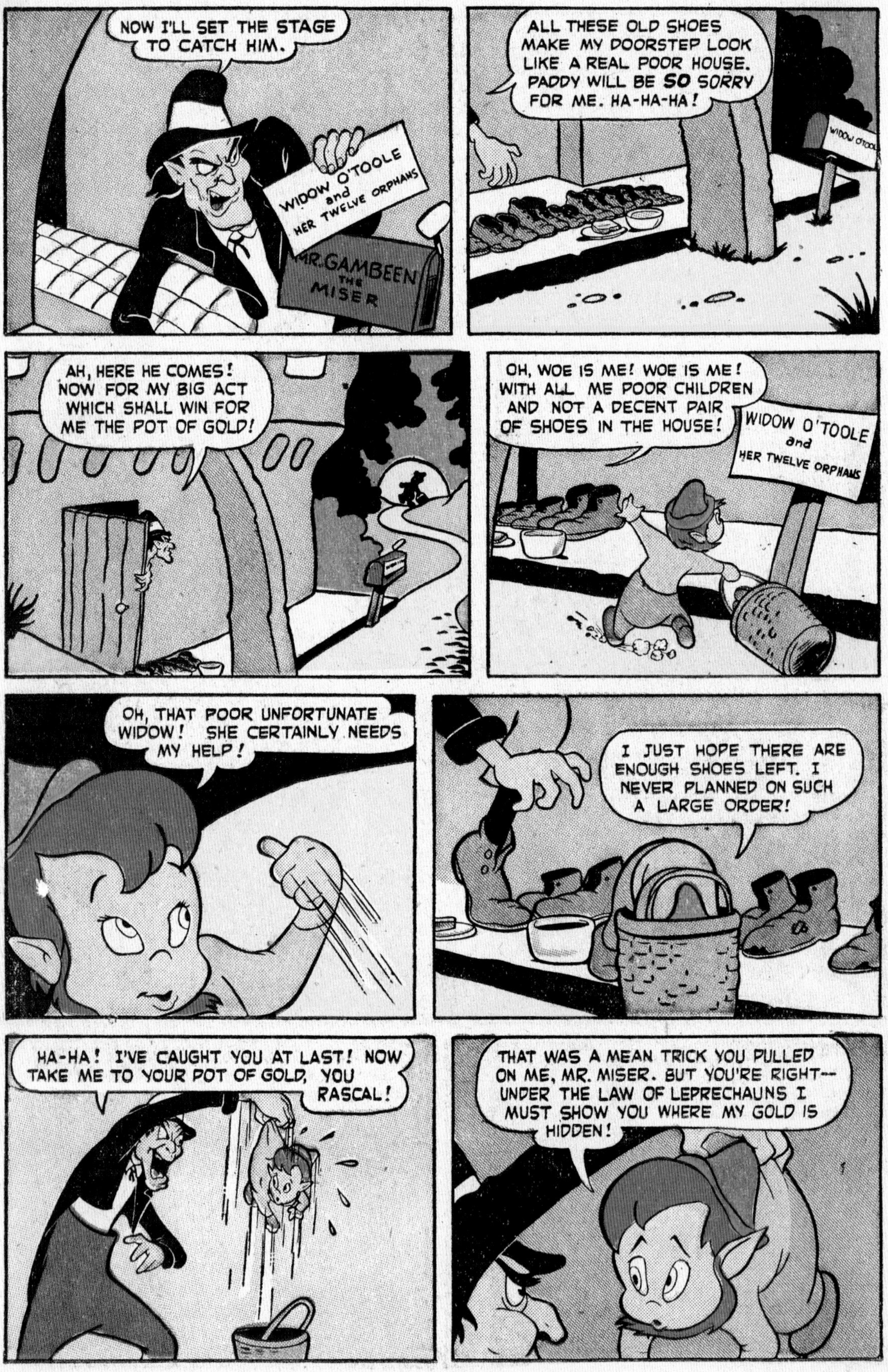
NOW I'LL SET THE STAGE TO CATCH HIM.
WIDOW O'TOOLE and HER TWELVE ORPHANS
MR. GAMBEEN THE MISER
ALL THESE OLD SHOES MAKE MY DOORSTEP LOOK LIKE A REAL POOR HOUSE. PADDY WILL BE **SO** SORRY FOR ME. HA-HA-HA!
WIDOW O'TOOLE
AH, HERE HE COMES! NOW FOR MY BIG ACT WHICH SHALL WIN FOR ME THE POT OF GOLD!
OH, WOE IS ME! WOE IS ME! WITH ALL ME POOR CHILDREN AND NOT A DECENT PAIR OF SHOES IN THE HOUSE!
WIDOW O'TOOLE and HER TWELVE ORPHANS
OH, THAT POOR UNFORTUNATE WIDOW! SHE CERTAINLY NEEDS MY HELP!
I JUST HOPE THERE ARE ENOUGH SHOES LEFT. I NEVER PLANNED ON SUCH A LARGE ORDER!
HA-HA! I'VE CAUGHT YOU AT LAST! NOW TAKE ME TO YOUR POT OF GOLD, YOU RASCAL!
THAT WAS A MEAN TRICK YOU PULLED ON ME, MR. MISER. BUT YOU'RE RIGHT-- UNDER THE LAW OF LEPRECHAUNS I MUST SHOW YOU WHERE MY GOLD IS HIDDEN!

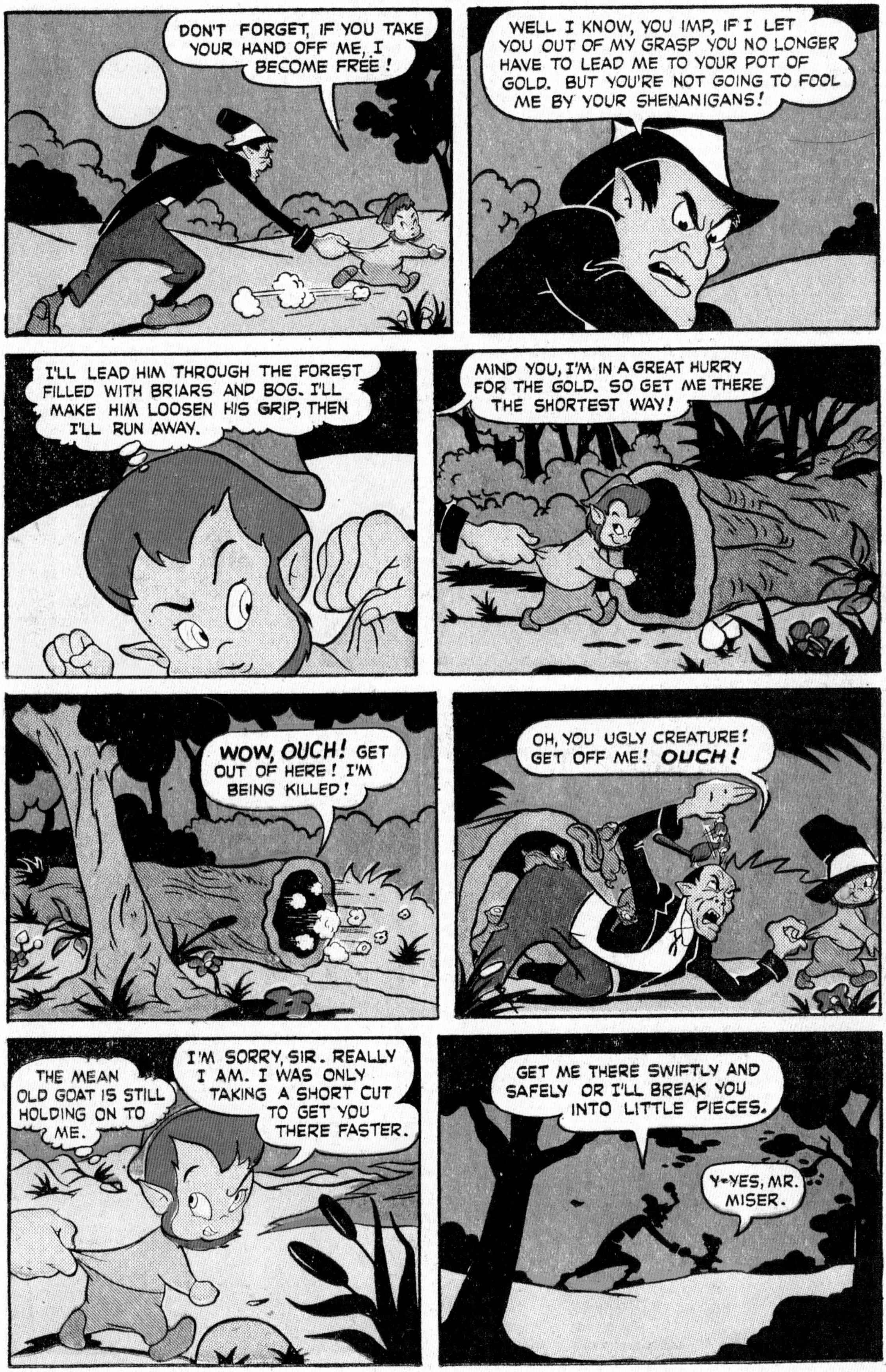
DON'T FORGET, IF YOU TAKE YOUR HAND OFF ME, I BECOME FREE!
WELL I KNOW, YOU IMP, IF I LET YOU OUT OF MY GRASP YOU NO LONGER HAVE TO LEAD ME TO YOUR POT OF GOLD. BUT YOU'RE NOT GOING TO FOOL ME BY YOUR SHENANIGANS!
I'LL LEAD HIM THROUGH THE FOREST FILLED WITH BRIARS AND BOG. I'LL MAKE HIM LOOSEN HIS GRIP, THEN I'LL RUN AWAY.
MIND YOU, I'M IN A GREAT HURRY FOR THE GOLD. SO GET ME THERE THE SHORTEST WAY!
WOW, OUCH! GET OUT OF HERE! I'M BEING KILLED!
OH, YOU UGLY CREATURE! GET OFF ME! OUCH!
THE MEAN OLD GOAT IS STILL HOLDING ON TO ME.
I'M SORRY, SIR. REALLY I AM. I WAS ONLY TAKING A SHORT CUT TO GET YOU THERE FASTER.
GET ME THERE SWIFTLY AND SAFELY OR I'LL BREAK YOU INTO LITTLE PIECES.
Y-YES, MR. MISER.

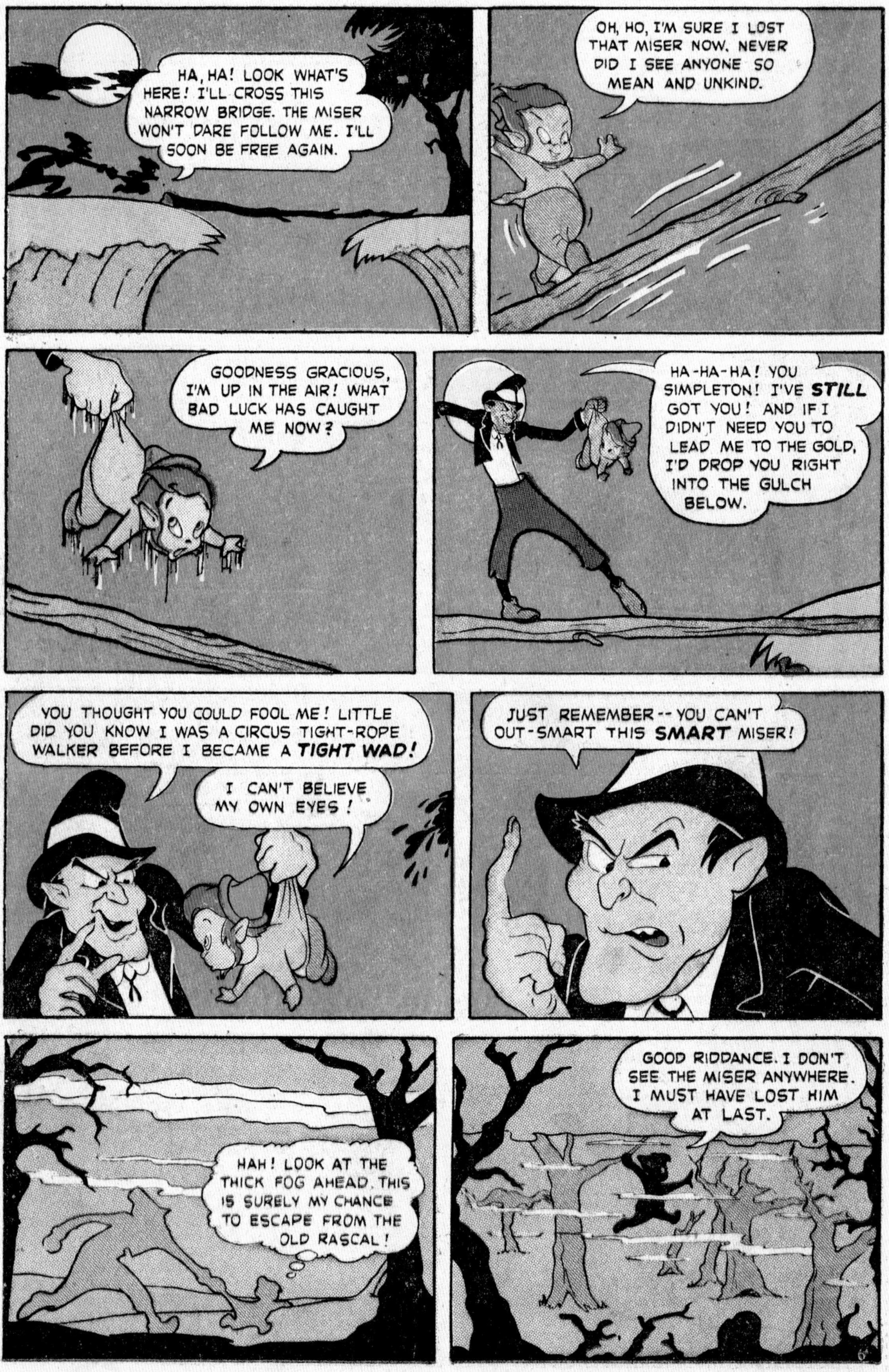
HA, HA! LOOK WHAT'S HERE! I'LL CROSS THIS NARROW BRIDGE. THE MISER WON'T DARE FOLLOW ME. I'LL SOON BE FREE AGAIN.
OH, HO, I'M SURE I LOST THAT MISER NOW. NEVER DID I SEE ANYONE SO MEAN AND UNKIND.
GOODNESS GRACIOUS, I'M UP IN THE AIR! WHAT BAD LUCK HAS CAUGHT ME NOW?
HA-HA-HA! YOU SIMPLETON! I'VE STILL GOT YOU! AND IF I DIDN'T NEED YOU TO LEAD ME TO THE GOLD, I'D DROP YOU RIGHT INTO THE GULCH BELOW.
YOU THOUGHT YOU COULD FOOL ME! LITTLE DID YOU KNOW I WAS A CIRCUS TIGHT-ROPE WALKER BEFORE I BECAME A TIGHT WAD!
I CAN'T BELIEVE MY OWN EYES!
JUST REMEMBER-- YOU CAN'T OUT-SMART THIS SMART MISER!
HAH! LOOK AT THE THICK FOG AHEAD. THIS IS SURELY MY CHANCE TO ESCAPE FROM THE OLD RASCAL!
GOOD RIDDANCE. I DON'T SEE THE MISER ANYWHERE. I MUST HAVE LOST HIM AT LAST.
6

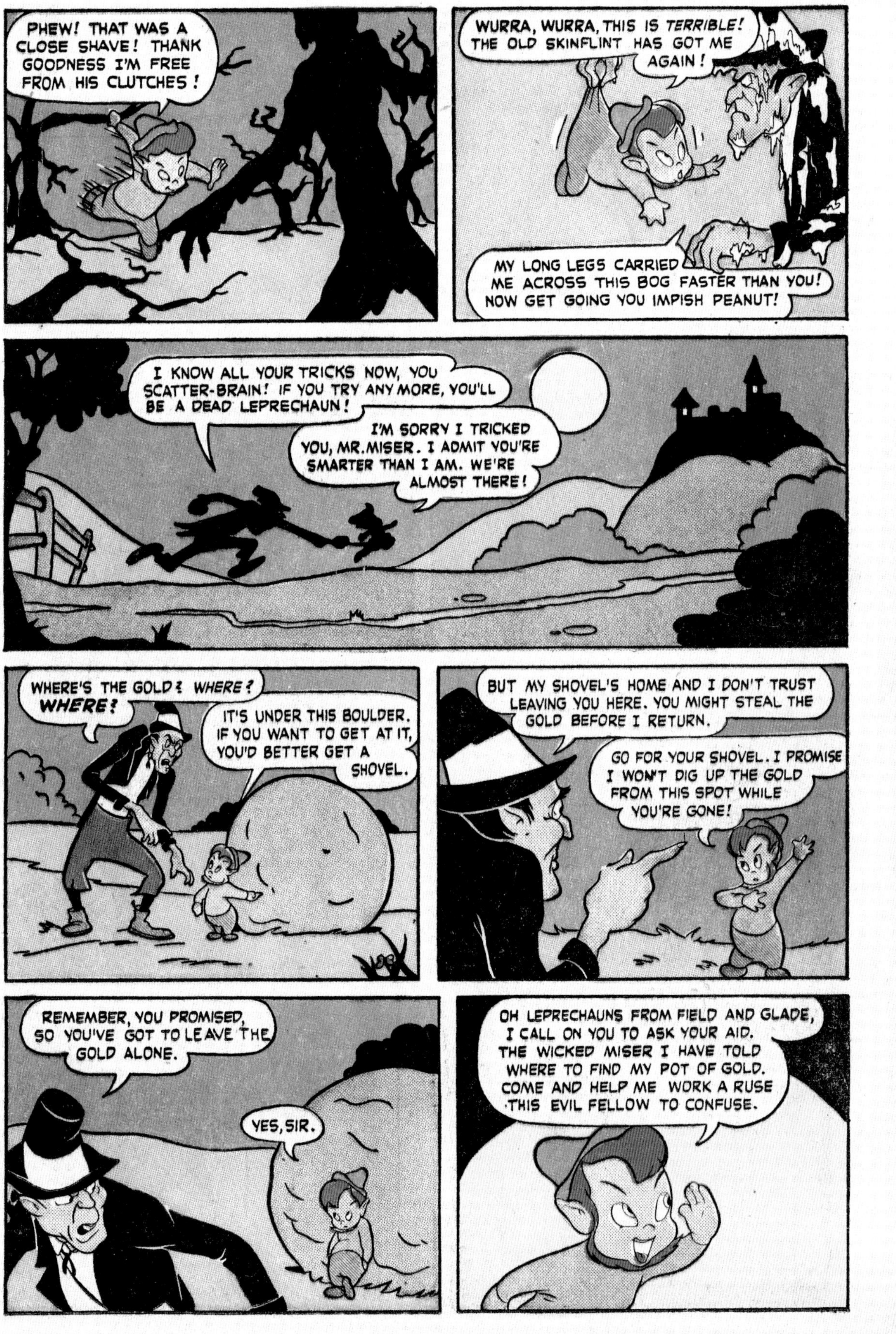
PHEW! THAT WAS A CLOSE SHAVE! THANK GOODNESS I'M FREE FROM HIS CLUTCHES!
WURRA, WURRA, THIS IS TERRIBLE! THE OLD SKINFLINT HAS GOT ME AGAIN!
MY LONG LEGS CARRIED ME ACROSS THIS BOG FASTER THAN YOU! NOW GET GOING YOU IMPISH PEANUT!
I KNOW ALL YOUR TRICKS NOW, YOU SCATTER-BRAIN! IF YOU TRY ANY MORE, YOU'LL BE A DEAD LEPRECHAUN!
I'M SORRY I TRICKED YOU, MR. MISER. I ADMIT YOU'RE SMARTER THAN I AM. WE'RE ALMOST THERE!
WHERE'S THE GOLD? WHERE? WHERE?
IT'S UNDER THIS BOULDER. IF YOU WANT TO GET AT IT, YOU'D BETTER GET A SHOVEL.
BUT MY SHOVEL'S HOME AND I DON'T TRUST LEAVING YOU HERE. YOU MIGHT STEAL THE GOLD BEFORE I RETURN.
GO FOR YOUR SHOVEL. I PROMISE I WON'T DIG UP THE GOLD FROM THIS SPOT WHILE YOU'RE GONE!
REMEMBER, YOU PROMISED, SO YOU'VE GOT TO LEAVE THE GOLD ALONE.
YES, SIR.
OH LEPRECHAUNS FROM FIELD AND GLADE, I CALL ON YOU TO ASK YOUR AID. THE WICKED MISER I HAVE TOLD WHERE TO FIND MY POT OF GOLD. COME AND HELP ME WORK A RUSE THIS EVIL FELLOW TO CONFUSE.

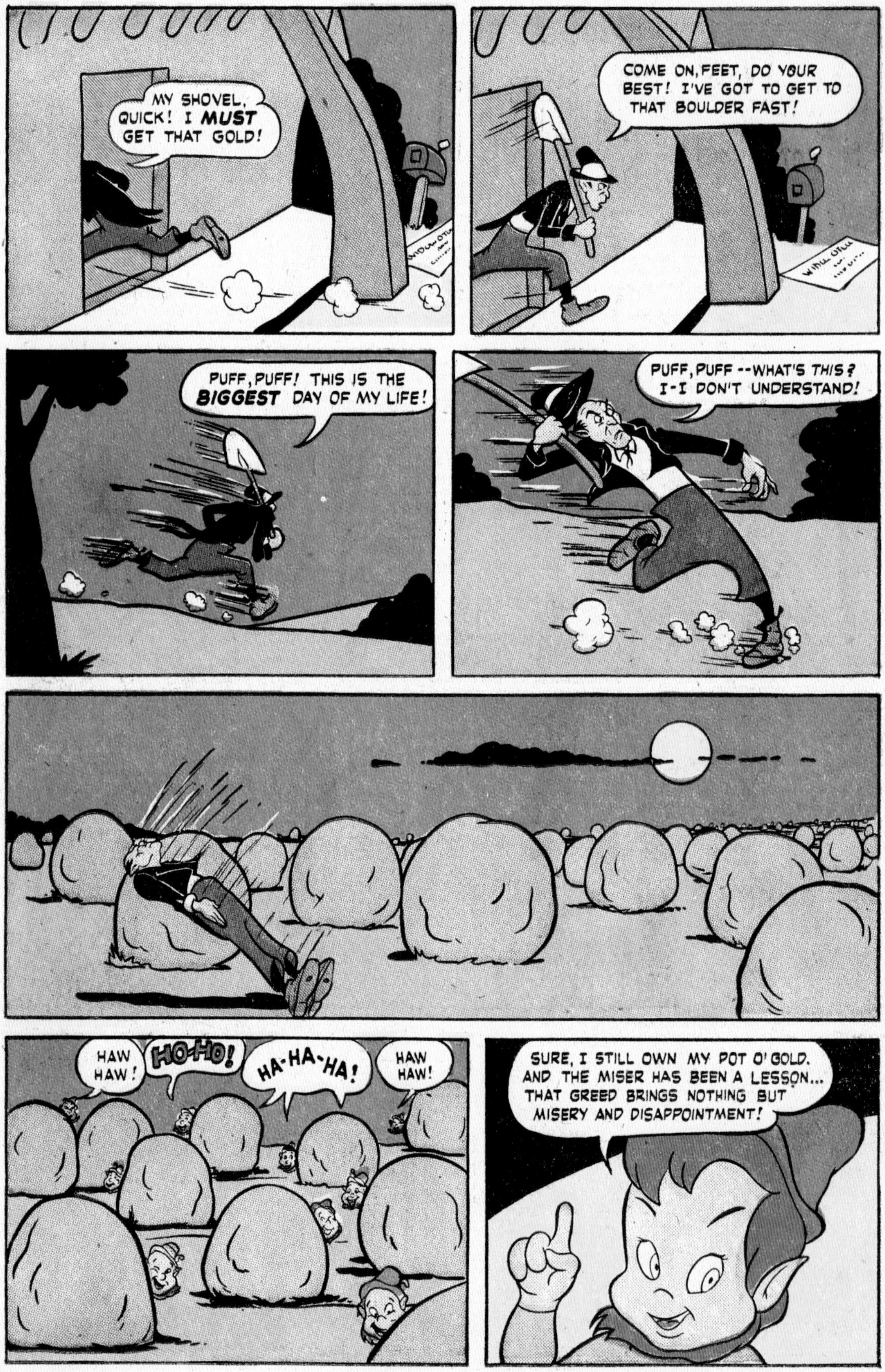
MY SHOVEL, QUICK! I MUST GET THAT GOLD!
COME ON, FEET, DO YOUR BEST! I'VE GOT TO GET TO THAT BOULDER FAST!
PUFF, PUFF! THIS IS THE BIGGEST DAY OF MY LIFE!
PUFF, PUFF --WHAT'S THIS? I-I DON'T UNDERSTAND!
HAW HAW!
HO-HO!
HA-HA-HA!
HAW HAW!
SURE, I STILL OWN MY POT O' GOLD. AND THE MISER HAS BEEN A LESSON... THAT GREED BRINGS NOTHING BUT MISERY AND DISAPPOINTMENT!

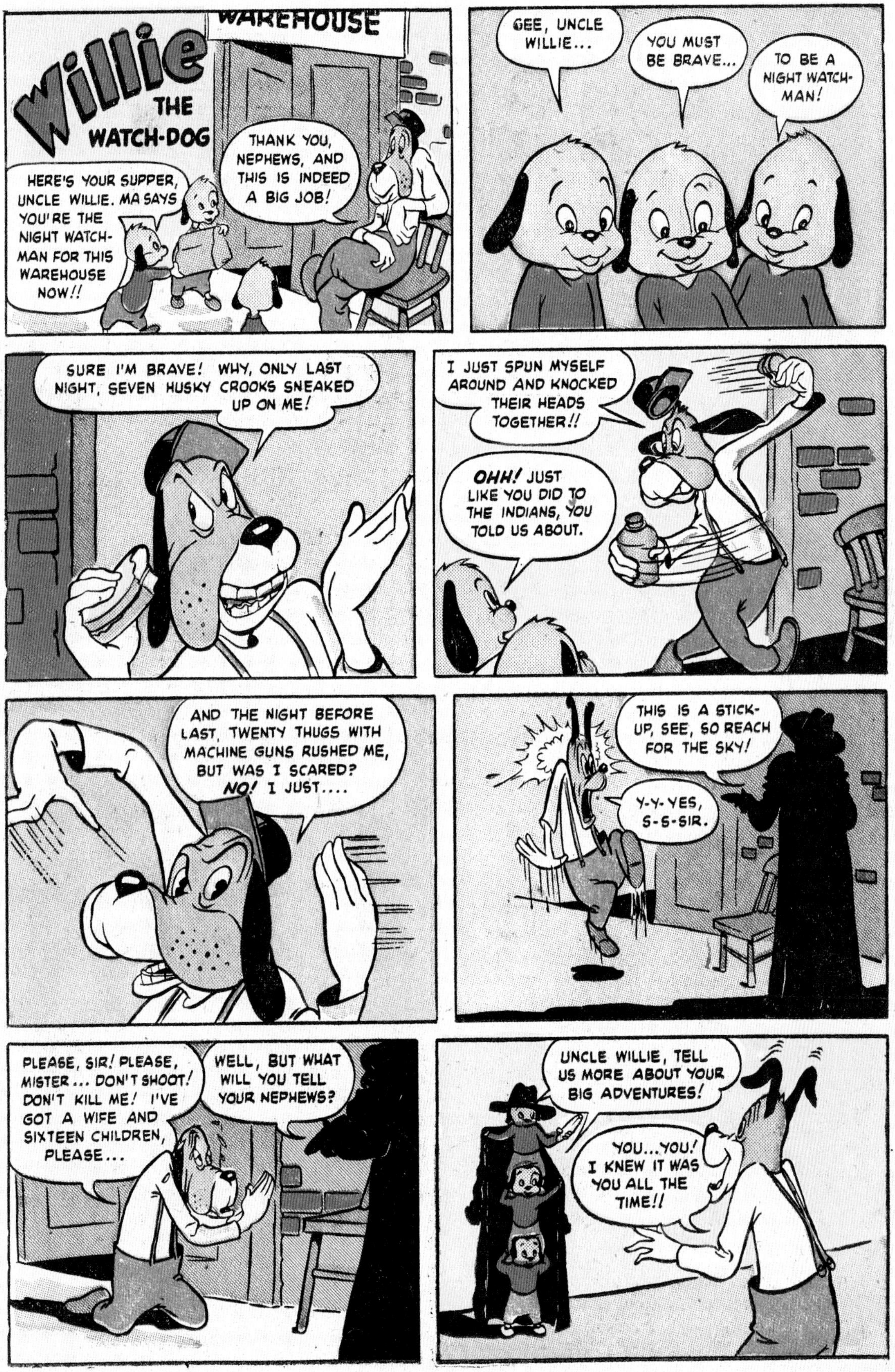
WAREHOUSE
Willie THE WATCH-DOG
HERE'S YOUR SUPPER, UNCLE WILLIE. MA SAYS YOU'RE THE NIGHT WATCH-MAN FOR THIS WAREHOUSE NOW!!
THANK YOU, NEPHEWS, AND THIS IS INDEED A BIG JOB!
GEE, UNCLE WILLIE...
YOU MUST BE BRAVE...
TO BE A NIGHT WATCH-MAN!
SURE I'M BRAVE! WHY, ONLY LAST NIGHT, SEVEN HUSKY CROOKS SNEAKED UP ON ME!
I JUST SPUN MYSELF AROUND AND KNOCKED THEIR HEADS TOGETHER!!
OHH! JUST LIKE YOU DID TO THE INDIANS, YOU TOLD US ABOUT.
AND THE NIGHT BEFORE LAST, TWENTY THUGS WITH MACHINE GUNS RUSHED ME, BUT WAS I SCARED? NO! I JUST....
THIS IS A STICK-UP, SEE, SO REACH FOR THE SKY!
Y-Y-YES, S-S-SIR.
PLEASE, SIR! PLEASE, MISTER... DON'T SHOOT! DON'T KILL ME! I'VE GOT A WIFE AND SIXTEEN CHILDREN, PLEASE...
WELL, BUT WHAT WILL YOU TELL YOUR NEPHEWS?
UNCLE WILLIE, TELL US MORE ABOUT YOUR BIG ADVENTURES!
YOU...YOU! I KNEW IT WAS YOU ALL THE TIME!!

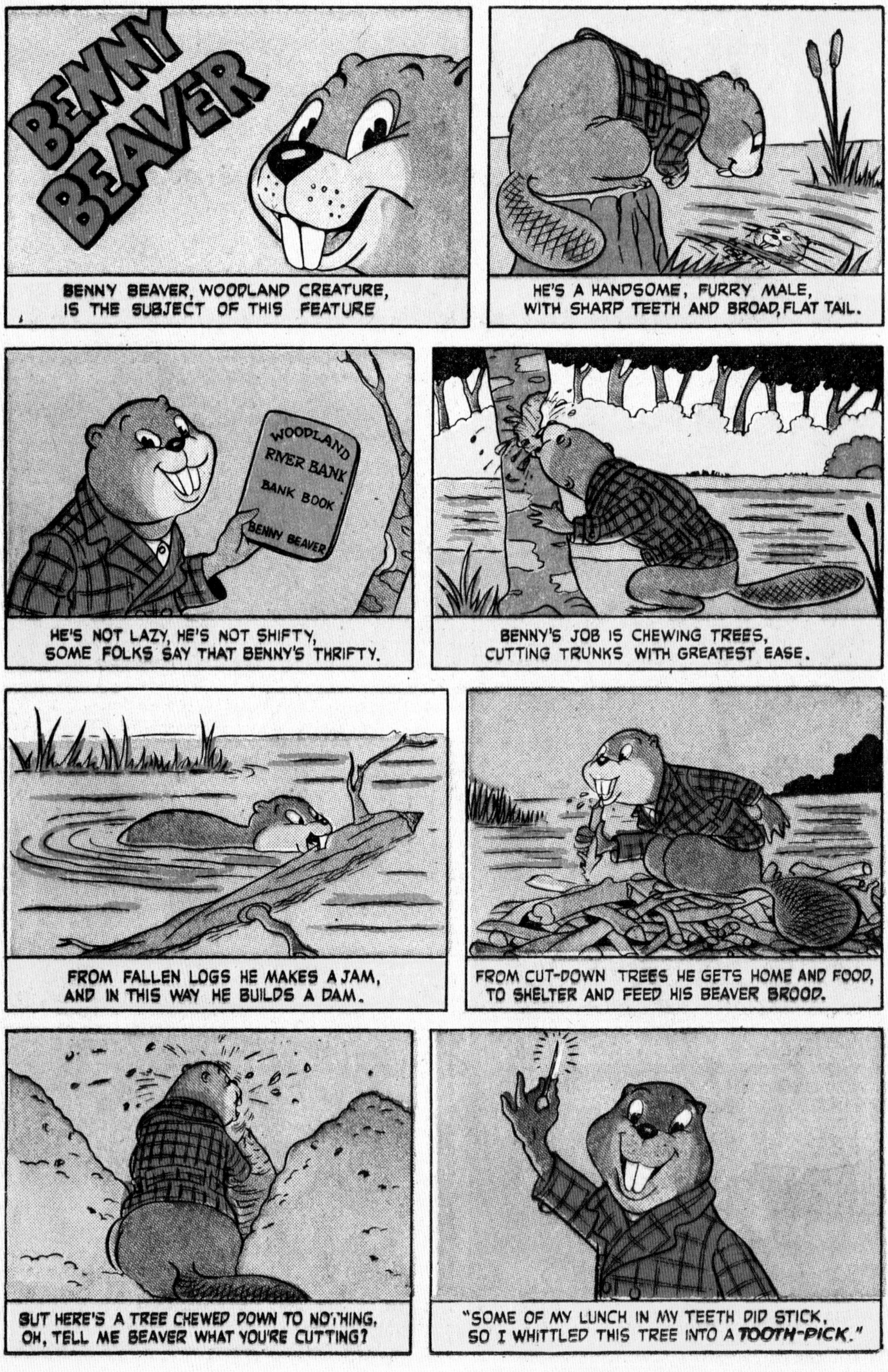
BENNY BEAVER
BENNY BEAVER, WOODLAND CREATURE, IS THE SUBJECT OF THIS FEATURE
HE'S A HANDSOME, FURRY MALE, WITH SHARP TEETH AND BROAD, FLAT TAIL.
WOODLAND RIVER BANK BANK BOOK BENNY BEAVER
HE'S NOT LAZY, HE'S NOT SHIFTY, SOME FOLKS SAY THAT BENNY'S THRIFTY.
BENNY'S JOB IS CHEWING TREES, CUTTING TRUNKS WITH GREATEST EASE.
FROM FALLEN LOGS HE MAKES A JAM, AND IN THIS WAY HE BUILDS A DAM.
FROM CUT-DOWN TREES HE GETS HOME AND FOOD, TO SHELTER AND FEED HIS BEAVER BROOD.
BUT HERE'S A TREE CHEWED DOWN TO NOTHING, OH, TELL ME BEAVER WHAT YOU'RE CUTTING?
"SOME OF MY LUNCH IN MY TEETH DID STICK, SO I WHITTLED THIS TREE INTO A TOOTH-PICK."

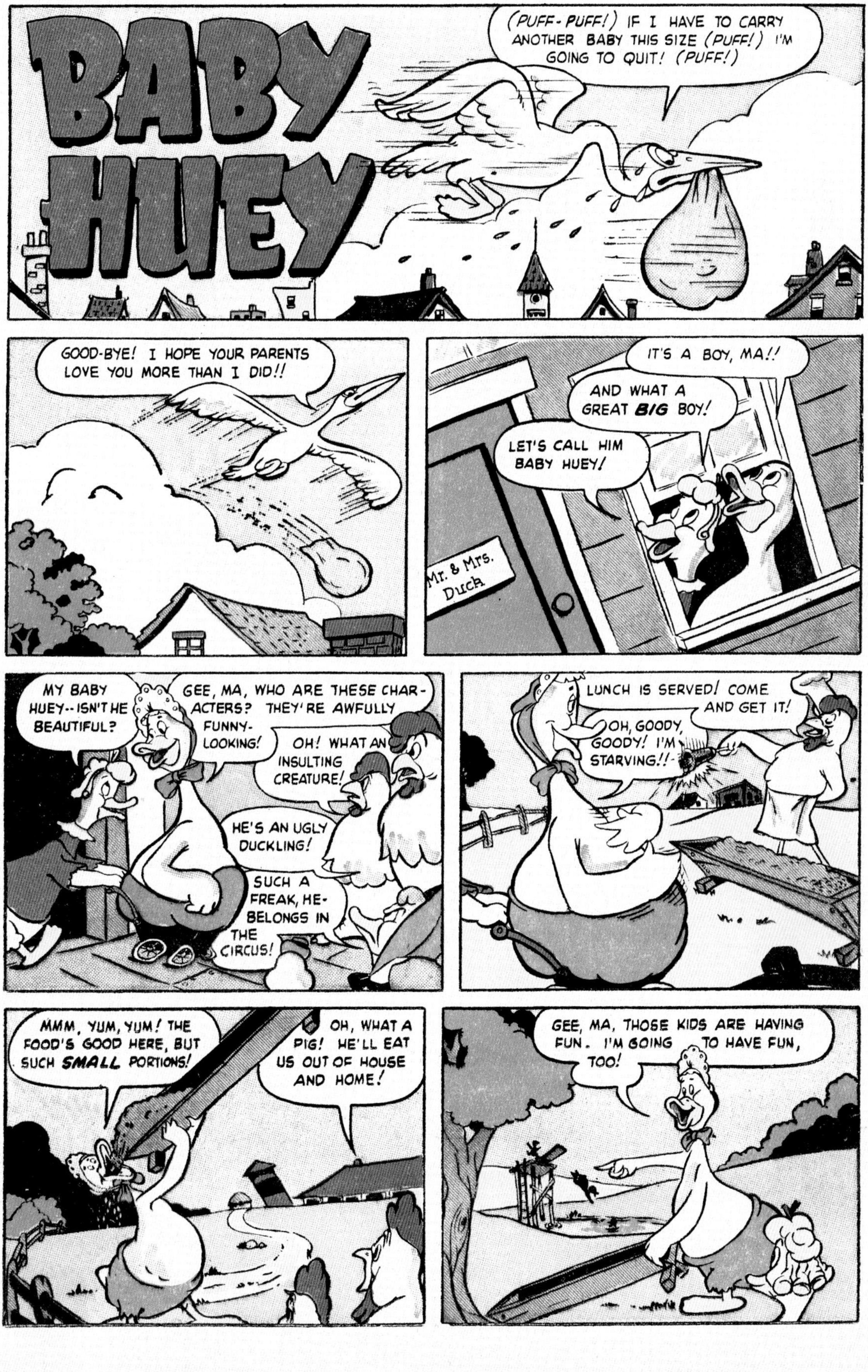
BABY HUEY
(PUFF-PUFF!) IF I HAVE TO CARRY ANOTHER BABY THIS SIZE (PUFF!) I'M GOING TO QUIT! (PUFF!)
GOOD-BYE! I HOPE YOUR PARENTS LOVE YOU MORE THAN I DID!!
IT'S A BOY, MA!!
AND WHAT A GREAT BIG BOY!
LET'S CALL HIM BABY HUEY!
Mr. & Mrs. Duck
MY BABY HUEY--ISN'T HE BEAUTIFUL?
GEE, MA, WHO ARE THESE CHAR-ACTERS? THEY'RE AWFULLY FUNNY-LOOKING!
OH! WHAT AN INSULTING CREATURE!
HE'S AN UGLY DUCKLING!
SUCH A FREAK, HE-BELONGS IN THE CIRCUS!
LUNCH IS SERVED! COME AND GET IT!
OH, GOODY, GOODY! I'M STARVING!!
MMM, YUM, YUM! THE FOOD'S GOOD HERE, BUT SUCH SMALL PORTIONS!
OH, WHAT A PIG! HE'LL EAT US OUT OF HOUSE AND HOME!
GEE, MA, THOSE KIDS ARE HAVING FUN. I'M GOING TO HAVE FUN, TOO!

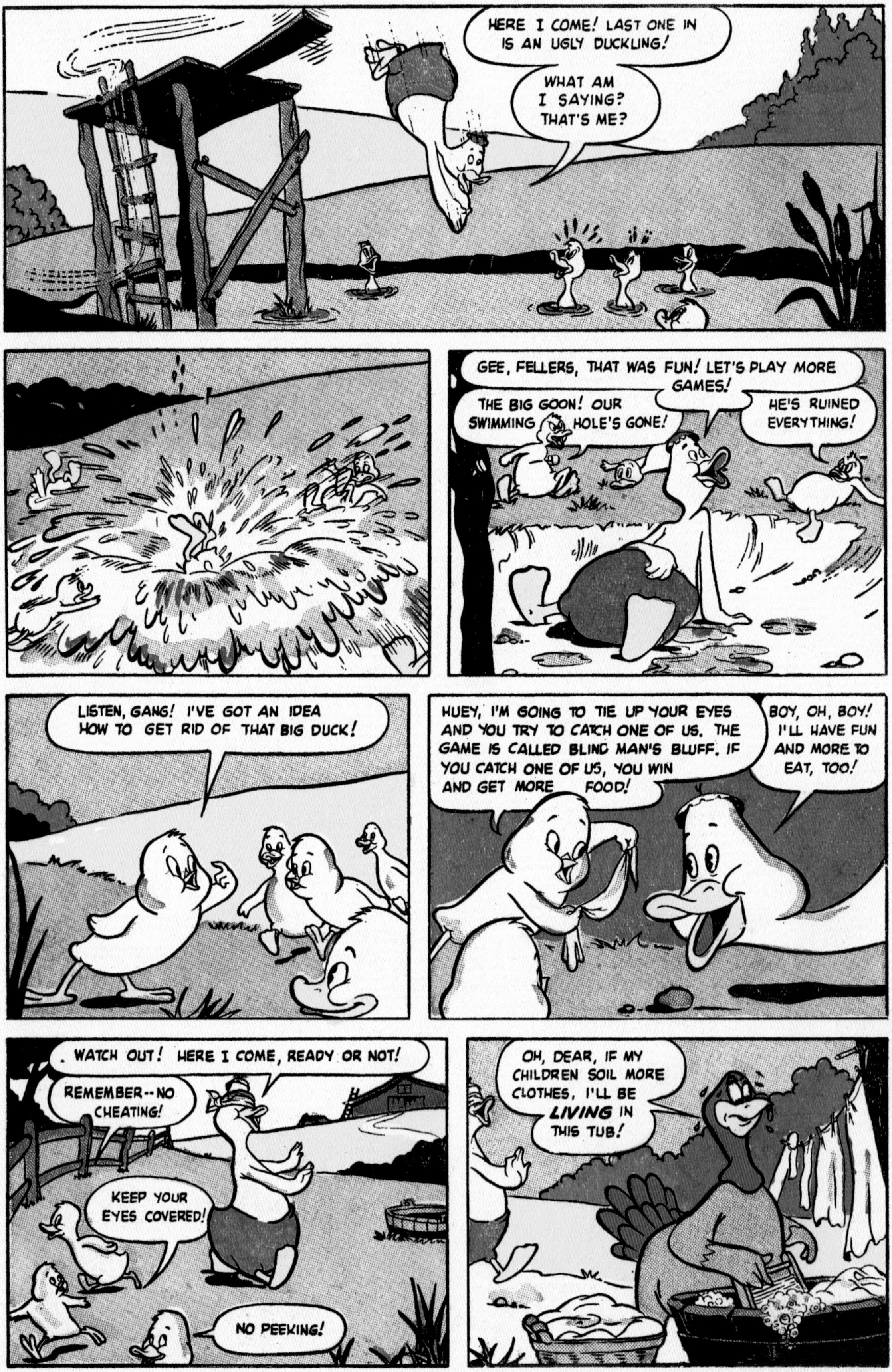
HERE I COME! LAST ONE IN IS AN UGLY DUCKLING!
WHAT AM I SAYING? THAT'S ME?
GEE, FELLERS, THAT WAS FUN! LET'S PLAY MORE GAMES!
THE BIG GOON! OUR SWIMMING HOLE'S GONE!
HE'S RUINED EVERYTHING!
LISTEN, GANG! I'VE GOT AN IDEA HOW TO GET RID OF THAT BIG DUCK!
HUEY, I'M GOING TO TIE UP YOUR EYES AND YOU TRY TO CATCH ONE OF US. THE GAME IS CALLED BLIND MAN'S BLUFF. IF YOU CATCH ONE OF US, YOU WIN AND GET MORE FOOD!
BOY, OH, BOY! I'LL HAVE FUN AND MORE TO EAT, TOO!
. WATCH OUT! HERE I COME, READY OR NOT!
REMEMBER--NO CHEATING!
KEEP YOUR EYES COVERED!
NO PEEKING!
OH, DEAR, IF MY CHILDREN SOIL MORE CLOTHES, I'LL BE LIVING IN THIS TUB!

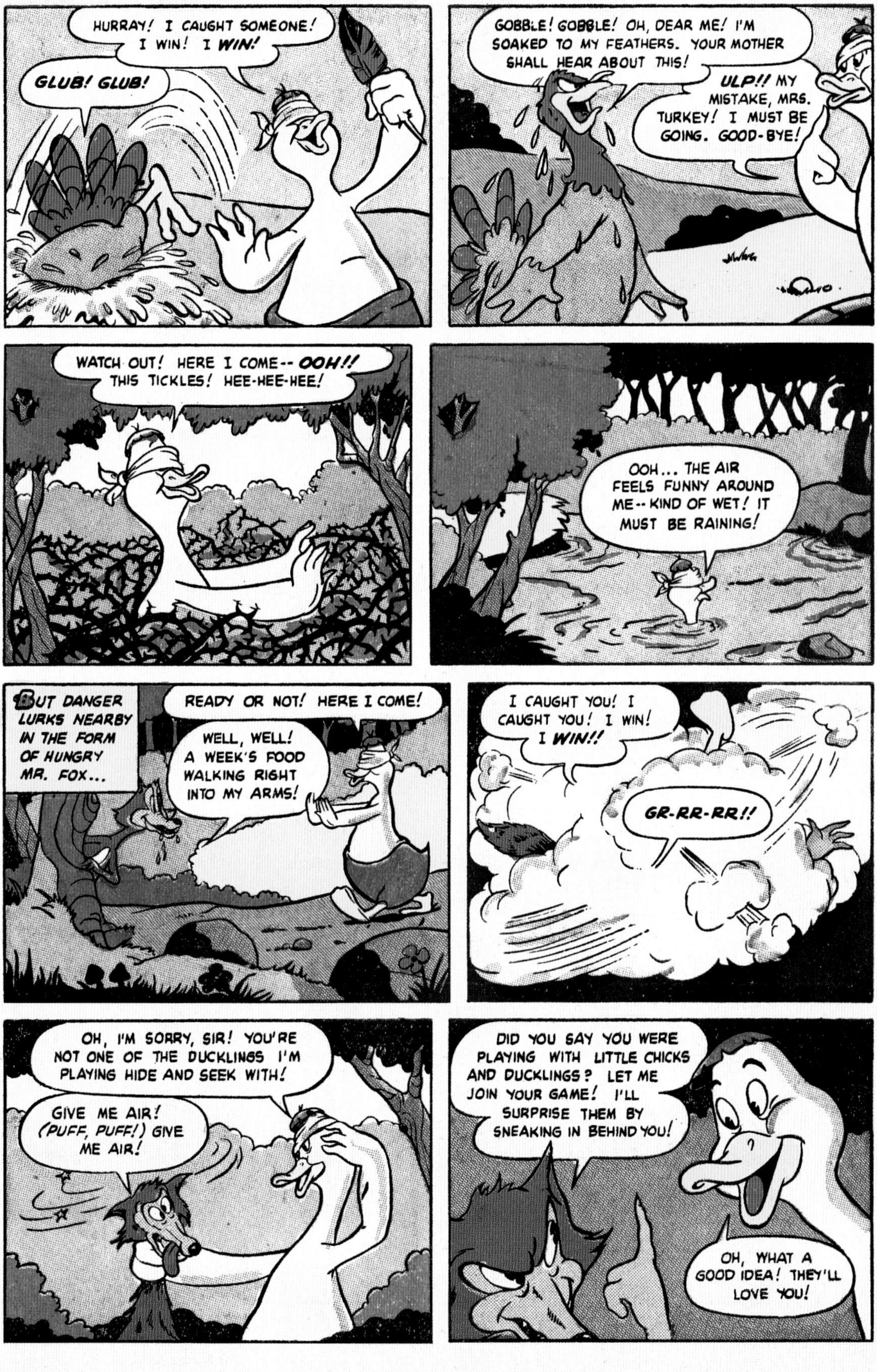
HURRAY! I CAUGHT SOMEONE! I WIN! I WIN!
GLUB! GLUB!
GOBBLE! GOBBLE! OH, DEAR ME! I'M SOAKED TO MY FEATHERS. YOUR MOTHER SHALL HEAR ABOUT THIS!
ULP!! MY MISTAKE, MRS. TURKEY! I MUST BE GOING. GOOD-BYE!
WATCH OUT! HERE I COME-- OOH!! THIS TICKLES! HEE-HEE-HEE!
OOH... THE AIR FEELS FUNNY AROUND ME-- KIND OF WET! IT MUST BE RAINING!
BUT DANGER LURKS NEARBY IN THE FORM OF HUNGRY MR. FOX...
READY OR NOT! HERE I COME!
WELL, WELL! A WEEK'S FOOD WALKING RIGHT INTO MY ARMS!
I CAUGHT YOU! I CAUGHT YOU! I WIN! I WIN!!
GR-RR-RR!!
OH, I'M SORRY, SIR! YOU'RE NOT ONE OF THE DUCKLINGS I'M PLAYING HIDE AND SEEK WITH!
GIVE ME AIR! (PUFF, PUFF!) GIVE ME AIR!
DID YOU SAY YOU WERE PLAYING WITH LITTLE CHICKS AND DUCKLINGS? LET ME JOIN YOUR GAME! I'LL SURPRISE THEM BY SNEAKING IN BEHIND YOU!
OH, WHAT A GOOD IDEA! THEY'LL LOVE YOU!

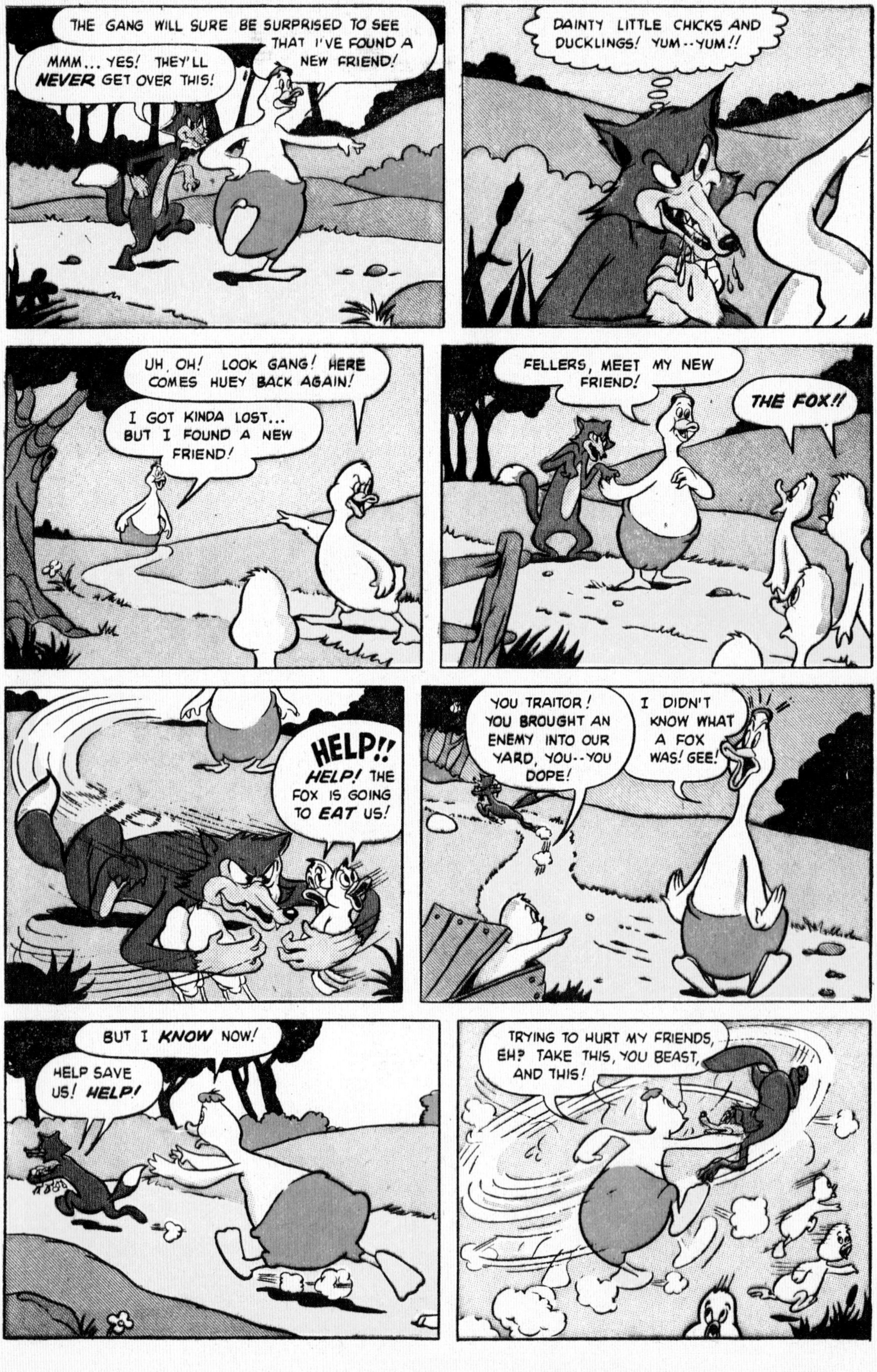
THE GANG WILL SURE BE SURPRISED TO SEE THAT I'VE FOUND A NEW FRIEND!
MMM... YES! THEY'LL NEVER GET OVER THIS!
DAINTY LITTLE CHICKS AND DUCKLINGS! YUM--YUM!!
UH, OH! LOOK GANG! HERE COMES HUEY BACK AGAIN!
I GOT KINDA LOST... BUT I FOUND A NEW FRIEND!
FELLERS, MEET MY NEW FRIEND!
THE FOX!!
HELP!! HELP! THE FOX IS GOING TO EAT US!
YOU TRAITOR! YOU BROUGHT AN ENEMY INTO OUR YARD, YOU--YOU DOPE!
I DIDN'T KNOW WHAT A FOX WAS! GEE!
BUT I KNOW NOW!
HELP SAVE US! HELP!
TRYING TO HURT MY FRIENDS, EH? TAKE THIS, YOU BEAST, AND THIS!

HURRAY FOR HUEY!

HUEY IS OUR HERO!

HURRAY! HURRAY!

THREE CHEERS FOR HUEY!!

HELP! I GIVE UP! HE'S THE WORLD'S CHAMPION FIGHTER!! HELP!

LOOK, MA, WHAT I'VE GOT! AIN'T IT PURTY?

HUEY, DON'T TELL ME YOU WERE OUT SHOPPING!

JUST THINK, AT HIS AGE, TO GIVE HIS MOTHER SUCH A BEAUTIFUL FOX FUR NECK PIECE!

OH, GEE, MA, THAT WAS NOTHING!

The End

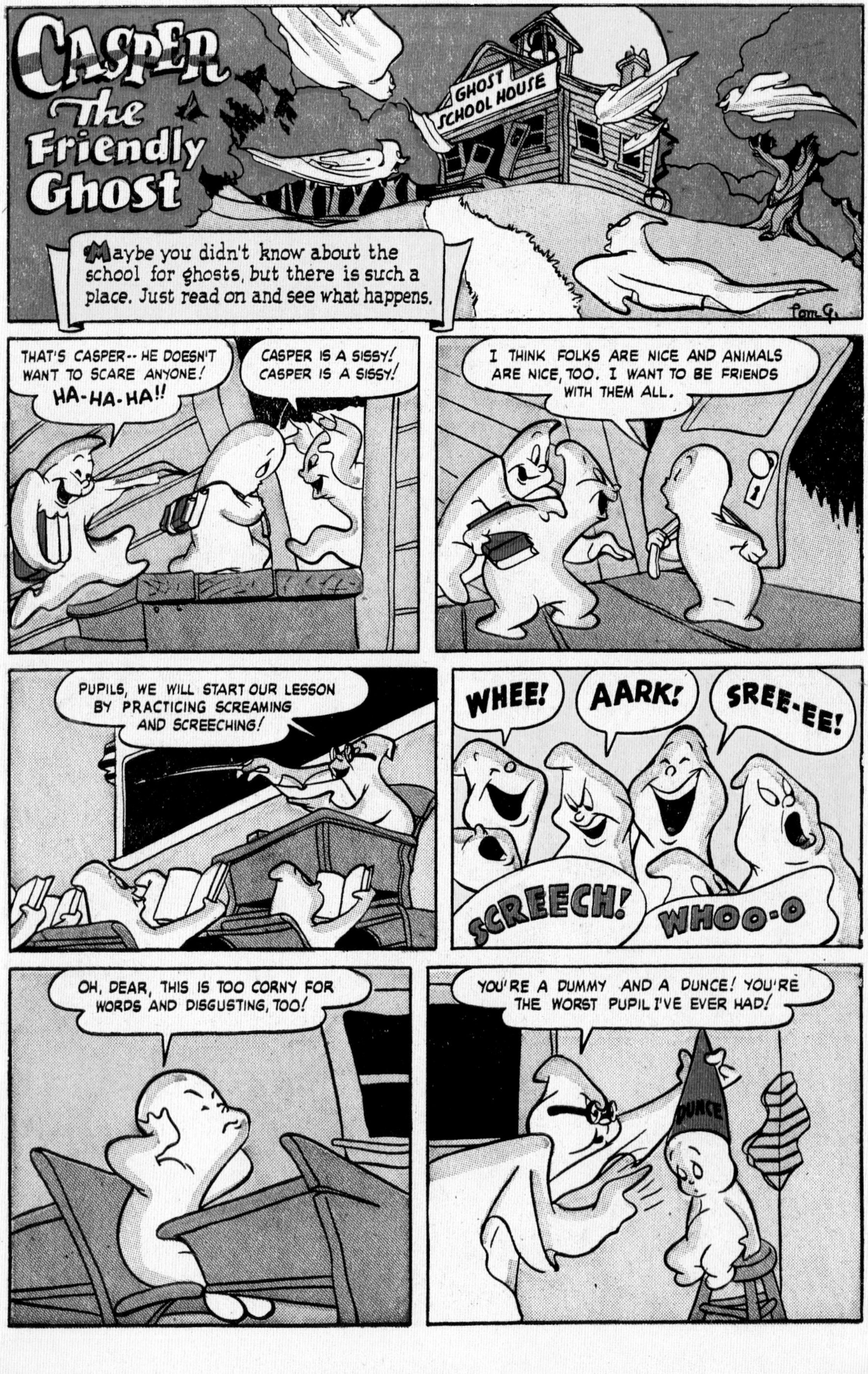

Casper The Friendly Ghost
GHOST SCHOOL HOUSE
Maybe you didn't know about the school for ghosts, but there is such a place. Just read on and see what happens.
THAT'S CASPER-- HE DOESN'T WANT TO SCARE ANYONE! HA-HA-HA!!
CASPER IS A SISSY! CASPER IS A SISSY!
I THINK FOLKS ARE NICE AND ANIMALS ARE NICE, TOO. I WANT TO BE FRIENDS WITH THEM ALL.
PUPILS, WE WILL START OUR LESSON BY PRACTICING SCREAMING AND SCREECHING!
WHEE!
AARK!
SREE-EE!
SCREECH!
WHOO-O
OH, DEAR, THIS IS TOO CORNY FOR WORDS AND DISGUSTING, TOO!
YOU'RE A DUMMY AND A DUNCE! YOU'RE THE WORST PUPIL I'VE EVER HAD!
DUNCE

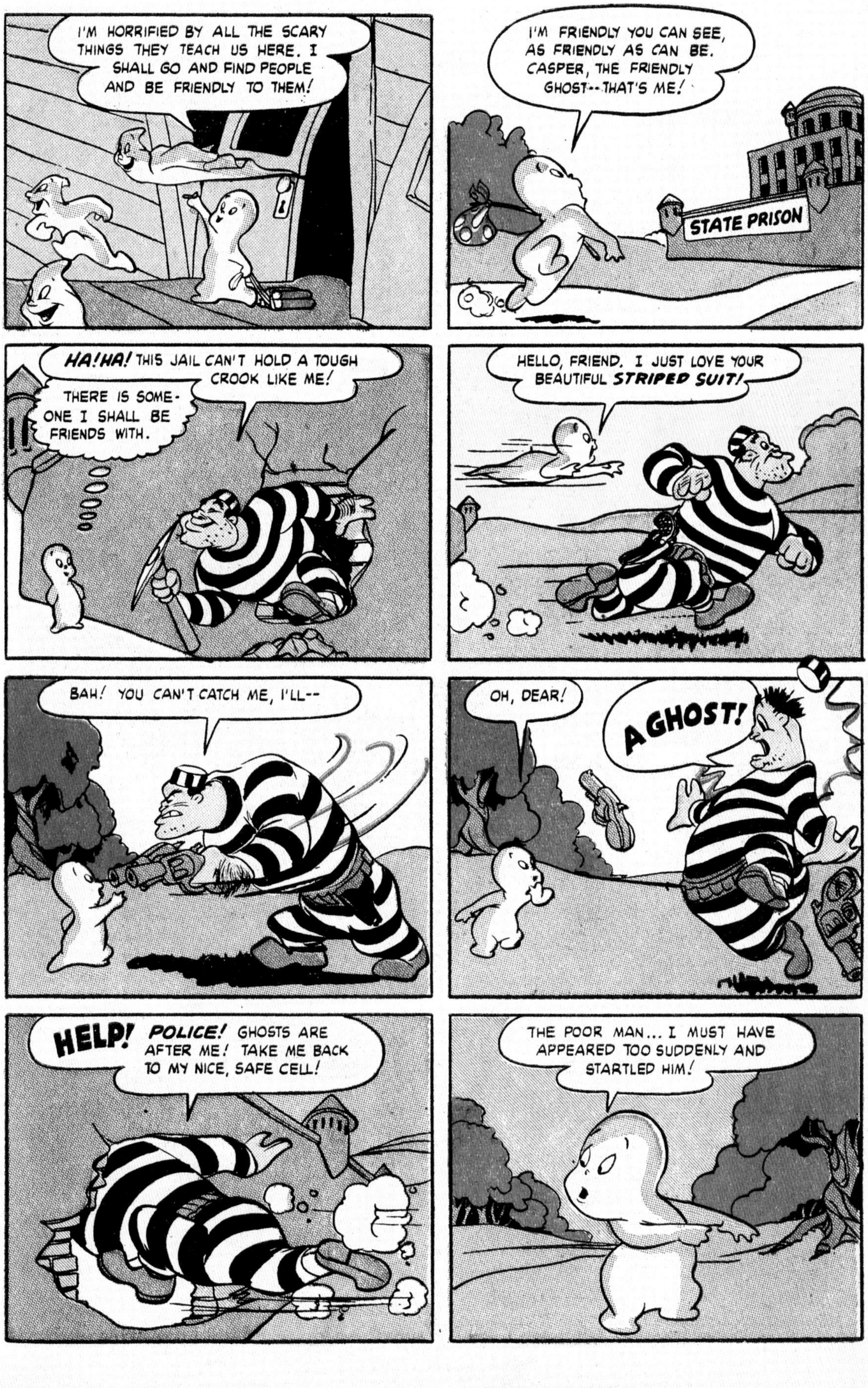
I'M HORRIFIED BY ALL THE SCARY THINGS THEY TEACH US HERE. I SHALL GO AND FIND PEOPLE AND BE FRIENDLY TO THEM!
I'M FRIENDLY YOU CAN SEE, AS FRIENDLY AS CAN BE. CASPER, THE FRIENDLY GHOST--THAT'S ME!
STATE PRISON
HA! HA! THIS JAIL CAN'T HOLD A TOUGH CROOK LIKE ME!
THERE IS SOME-ONE I SHALL BE FRIENDS WITH.
HELLO, FRIEND. I JUST LOVE YOUR BEAUTIFUL STRIPED SUIT!
BAH! YOU CAN'T CATCH ME, I'LL--
OH, DEAR!
A GHOST!
HELP! POLICE! GHOSTS ARE AFTER ME! TAKE ME BACK TO MY NICE, SAFE CELL!
THE POOR MAN... I MUST HAVE APPEARED TOO SUDDENLY AND STARTLED HIM!

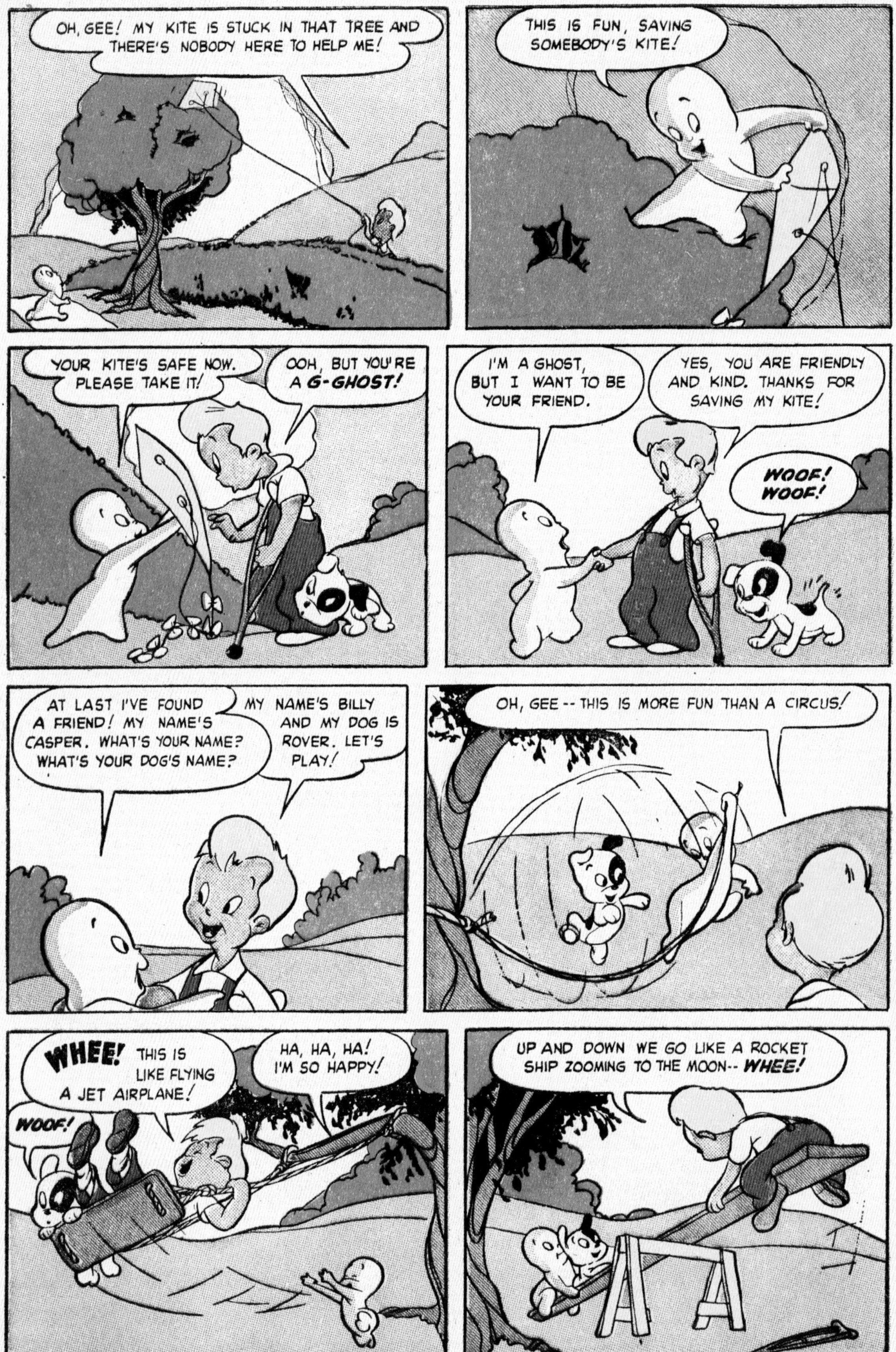
OH, GEE! MY KITE IS STUCK IN THAT TREE AND THERE'S NOBODY HERE TO HELP ME!
THIS IS FUN, SAVING SOMEBODY'S KITE!
YOUR KITE'S SAFE NOW. PLEASE TAKE IT!
OOH, BUT YOU'RE A G-GHOST!
I'M A GHOST, BUT I WANT TO BE YOUR FRIEND.
YES, YOU ARE FRIENDLY AND KIND. THANKS FOR SAVING MY KITE!
WOOF! WOOF!
AT LAST I'VE FOUND A FRIEND! MY NAME'S CASPER. WHAT'S YOUR NAME? WHAT'S YOUR DOG'S NAME?
MY NAME'S BILLY AND MY DOG IS ROVER. LET'S PLAY!
OH, GEE -- THIS IS MORE FUN THAN A CIRCUS!
WHEE! THIS IS LIKE FLYING A JET AIRPLANE!
HA, HA, HA! I'M SO HAPPY!
WOOF!
UP AND DOWN WE GO LIKE A ROCKET SHIP ZOOMING TO THE MOON-- WHEE!

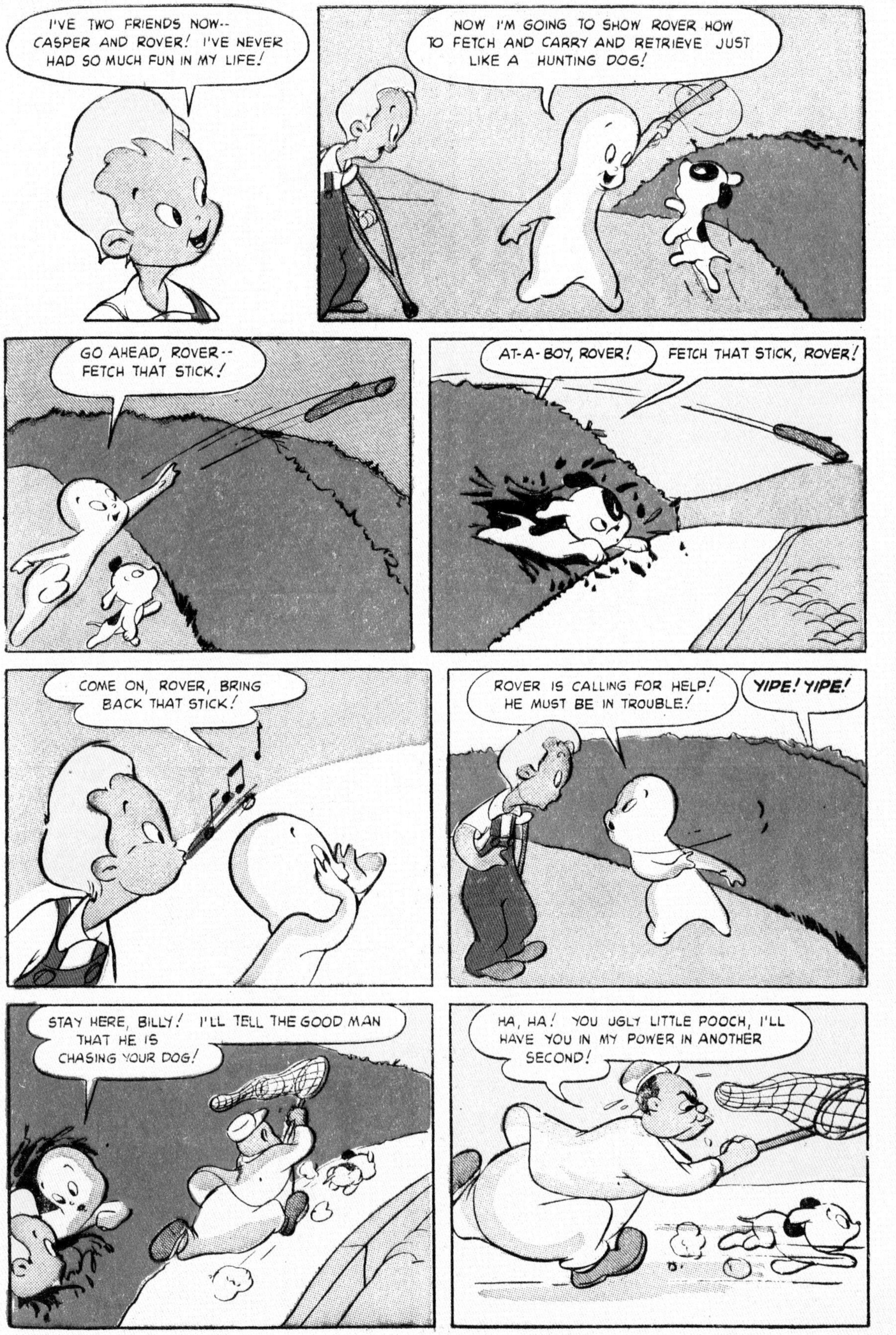
I'VE TWO FRIENDS NOW-- CASPER AND ROVER! I'VE NEVER HAD SO MUCH FUN IN MY LIFE!
NOW I'M GOING TO SHOW ROVER HOW TO FETCH AND CARRY AND RETRIEVE JUST LIKE A HUNTING DOG!
GO AHEAD, ROVER-- FETCH THAT STICK!
AT-A-BOY, ROVER!
FETCH THAT STICK, ROVER!
COME ON, ROVER, BRING BACK THAT STICK!
ROVER IS CALLING FOR HELP! HE MUST BE IN TROUBLE!
YIPE! YIPE!
STAY HERE, BILLY! I'LL TELL THE GOOD MAN THAT HE IS CHASING YOUR DOG!
HA, HA! YOU UGLY LITTLE POOCH, I'LL HAVE YOU IN MY POWER IN ANOTHER SECOND!

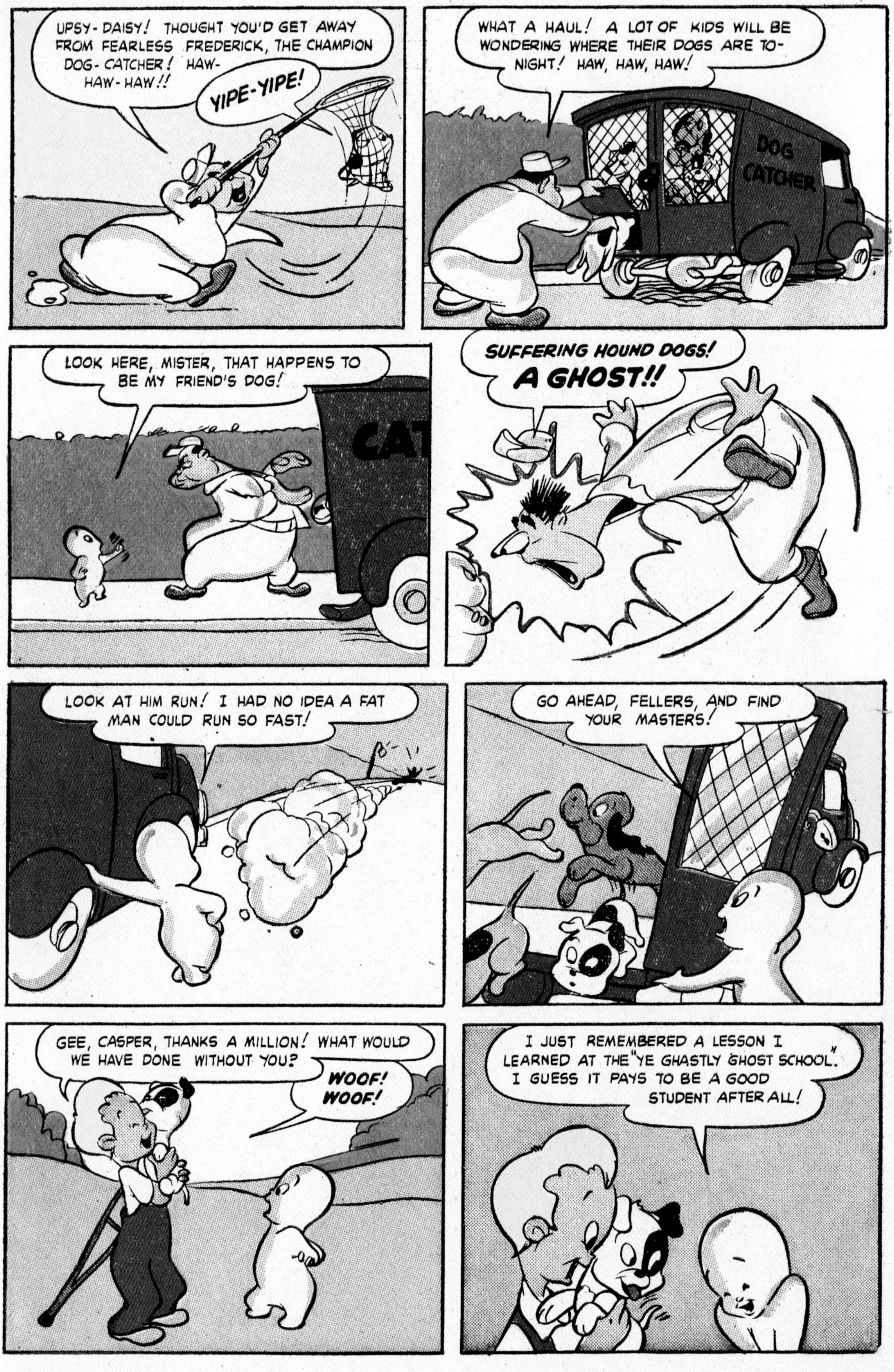
UPSY-DAISY! THOUGHT YOU'D GET AWAY FROM FEARLESS FREDERICK, THE CHAMPION DOG-CATCHER! HAW-HAW-HAW!!
YIPE-YIPE!
WHAT A HAUL! A LOT OF KIDS WILL BE WONDERING WHERE THEIR DOGS ARE TO-NIGHT! HAW, HAW, HAW!
DOG CATCHER
LOOK HERE, MISTER, THAT HAPPENS TO BE MY FRIEND'S DOG!
SUFFERING HOUND DOGS! A GHOST!!
LOOK AT HIM RUN! I HAD NO IDEA A FAT MAN COULD RUN SO FAST!
GO AHEAD, FELLERS, AND FIND YOUR MASTERS!
GEE, CASPER, THANKS A MILLION! WHAT WOULD WE HAVE DONE WITHOUT YOU?
WOOF! WOOF!
I JUST REMEMBERED A LESSON I LEARNED AT THE "YE GHASTLY GHOST SCHOOL." I GUESS IT PAYS TO BE A GOOD STUDENT AFTER ALL!

box that appeared to have been pried open with a hickory twig that lay splintered beside it. The back door was open, and the sheriff reckoned that the scoundrel had used it in making his escape.

Sure enough, in the mud outside the back door Sheriff Tick found fresh footprints that couldn't by any stretch of circumstances have been made by the victim or any of his neighbors. The sheriff measured the clearest print with a tape rule and judged that it had been made by a size .0009 shoe.

After a brief word with Chad Chigger, the coroner, the sheriff mounted Jasper who was champing on his bit and buzzed off through the misty darkness for the cobbler's shop.

Pounding loudly on the door, the sheriff finally aroused Crick Crickett who stumbled downstairs in nightgown and slippers to admit Creepy Town's champion of law and order. "What's the trouble?" Crick chirped in a frightened voice.

"What suspicious character around this town wears a size .0009 shoe?" the sheriff demanded. "Sam Centipede was stabbed in the back with a rose thorn by a bug thug who afterward made off with Sam's hoard of cash. An out-and-out case of homi — er, I mean insecticide. The culprit must be brought to justice!"

"Oooooh!" Crick wailed, holding his head. "That cancels the biggest order I ever received since I opened this shop. "Poor Sam! The crook who stabbed him must have known he had been saving money to buy fifty pairs of shoes. Size .0009, you said, Sheriff? Why, sure! Rod Roach wears that size. You might find Roach asleep outside. But watch out, Sheriff. Roach is quick on the trigger!"

"I'll keep an eye out for him," the sheriff said as he turned to leave, "but you can bet your last dollar that I won't find Roach asleep if he's guilty."

But Roach was asleep outside, curled up in an old thistledown blanket. The sheriff tapped him none too gently with the but of his gun, for he had reason to suspect that Roach might have tried to pull a fast one.

"Get up, you!" the sheriff snarled. "Let's see what size shoes you're wearing."

Rod Roach opened his eyes slowly and rolled to his feet. The sheriff looked down and saw that Roach was barefooted. "A wise guy, eh?" the sheriff snarled. "Trying to hide the evidence!"

"I don't know what you're talking about, Sheriff!" Rod Roach rasped. "If it's my shoes you're worried about, I left 'em over to Crick Crickett's yesterday to be repaired. Now let me go back to sleep!"

Sheriff Tick muttered and turned on his heels. "Something's screwy!" he thought. "Why didn't Roach wait while his shoes were being repaired? Why did he leave them overnight at the cobbler's? Aha! I've got it! But this is going to take some careful sleuthing!"

Leaving Jasper at the hitching rail outside the post office, Sheriff Tick took a roundabout route through dark alleys and backyards to the ant stable across the street from the cobbler's shop. Thumbing the cylinder of his gun nervously, he stood in the shadows watching Crickett's establishment. Crick had gone back up to bed, and the shop was dark.

Suddenly from out of the gloom a furtive figure appeared. On tiptoes he made his way toward the cobbler's shop, and paused for a moment outside the door before he slipped a key into the lock. Sheriff Tick didn't recognize him at first, but saw that he was barefooted and carrying a pair of shoes. The moment the figure stepped into the shop, Sheriff Tick dashed across the street. And when Deedee Tee stepped out, he was looking straight into the muzzle of the sheriff's gun.

"I — I didn't do it, Sheriff!" he croaked. "I just stole Rod's shoes from here earlier in the evening, but my conscience bothered me so I brought them back."

"After you stabbed Sam Centipede and made off with his money!" the sheriff snarled. "You stole Rod's shoes to make it look like he was guilty. Let me search you!"

Deedee Tee knew that the sheriff would shoot him down like a dog flea if he tried to make a break. Trembling, he obeyed the order.

Keeping the gun pressed against Deedee's ribs, the sheriff went through the crook's pockets. Five seconds later the doorway was green with looted money.

"Caught with the goods!" Sheriff Tick growled. "You'll hang for this, Deedee Tee!"

Suddenly Jim Crickett was in the doorway. "Well, I'll be hanged, too, Sheriff! I plumb forgot that Rod had left his shoes to be tapped!"

As the sheriff slipped handcuffs on the prisoner and turned to drag him away, he threw a mean look back at the cobbler and muttered under his breath: "Yeah? *You* ought to be tapped, too, Crickett!"

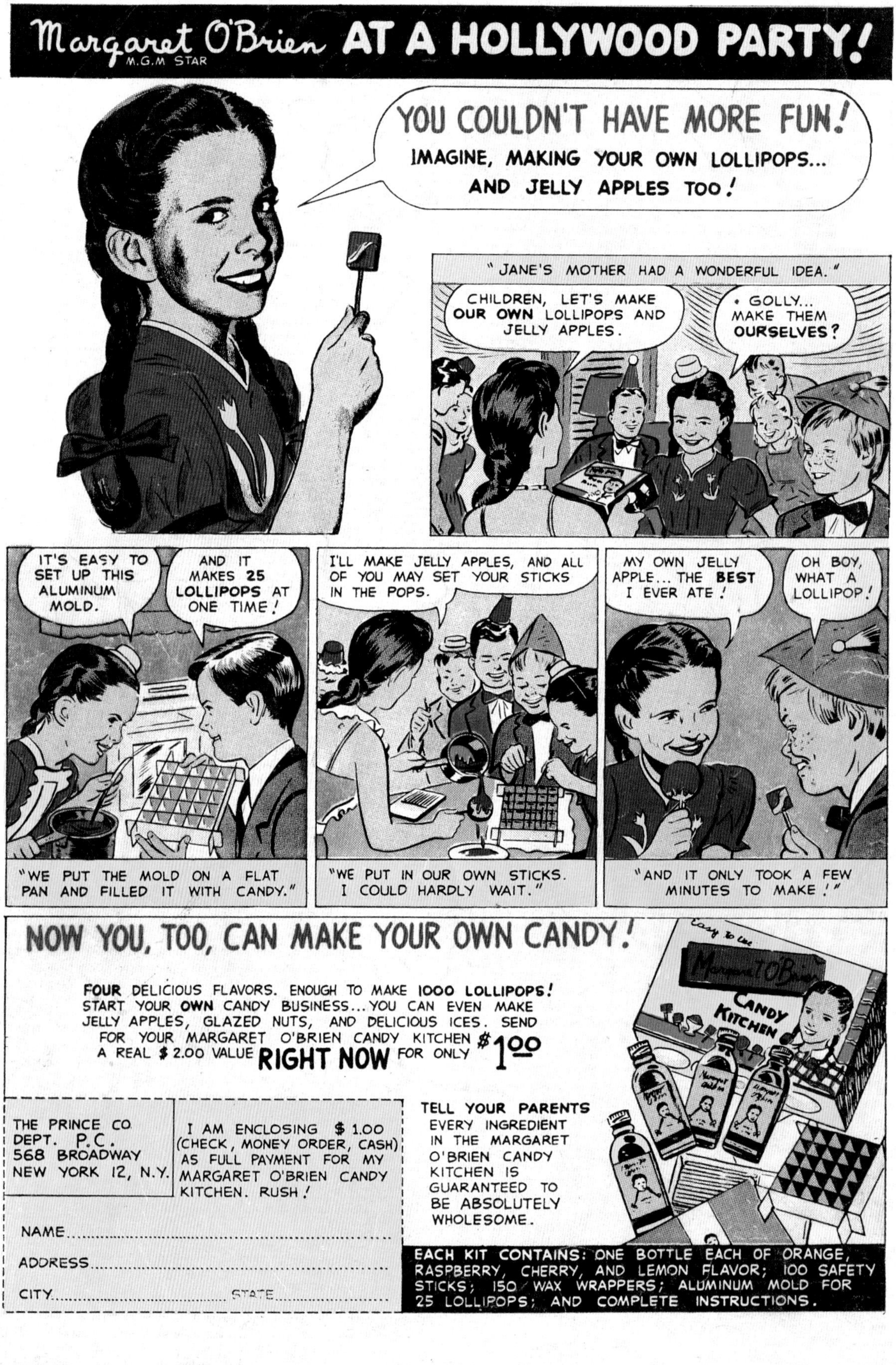
Margaret O'Brien M.G.M STAR AT A HOLLYWOOD PARTY!
YOU COULDN'T HAVE MORE FUN!
IMAGINE, MAKING YOUR OWN LOLLIPOPS... AND JELLY APPLES TOO!
"JANE'S MOTHER HAD A WONDERFUL IDEA."
CHILDREN, LET'S MAKE OUR OWN LOLLIPOPS AND JELLY APPLES.
GOLLY... MAKE THEM OURSELVES?
IT'S EASY TO SET UP THIS ALUMINUM MOLD.
AND IT MAKES 25 LOLLIPOPS AT ONE TIME!
"WE PUT THE MOLD ON A FLAT PAN AND FILLED IT WITH CANDY."
I'LL MAKE JELLY APPLES, AND ALL OF YOU MAY SET YOUR STICKS IN THE POPS.
"WE PUT IN OUR OWN STICKS. I COULD HARDLY WAIT."
MY OWN JELLY APPLE... THE BEST I EVER ATE!
OH BOY, WHAT A LOLLIPOP!
"AND IT ONLY TOOK A FEW MINUTES TO MAKE!"
NOW YOU, TOO, CAN MAKE YOUR OWN CANDY!
FOUR DELICIOUS FLAVORS. ENOUGH TO MAKE 1000 LOLLIPOPS! START YOUR OWN CANDY BUSINESS... YOU CAN EVEN MAKE JELLY APPLES, GLAZED NUTS, AND DELICIOUS ICES. SEND FOR YOUR MARGARET O'BRIEN CANDY KITCHEN A REAL $ 2.00 VALUE RIGHT NOW FOR ONLY $1.00
Easy to use Margaret O'Brien CANDY KITCHEN
THE PRINCE CO DEPT. P.C. 568 BROADWAY NEW YORK 12, N.Y.
I AM ENCLOSING $ 1.00 (CHECK, MONEY ORDER, CASH) AS FULL PAYMENT FOR MY MARGARET O'BRIEN CANDY KITCHEN. RUSH!
NAME
ADDRESS
CITY
STATE
TELL YOUR PARENTS EVERY INGREDIENT IN THE MARGARET O'BRIEN CANDY KITCHEN IS GUARANTEED TO BE ABSOLUTELY WHOLESOME.
EACH KIT CONTAINS: ONE BOTTLE EACH OF ORANGE, RASPBERRY, CHERRY, AND LEMON FLAVOR; 100 SAFETY STICKS; 150 WAX WRAPPERS; ALUMINUM MOLD FOR 25 LOLLIPOPS; AND COMPLETE INSTRUCTIONS.

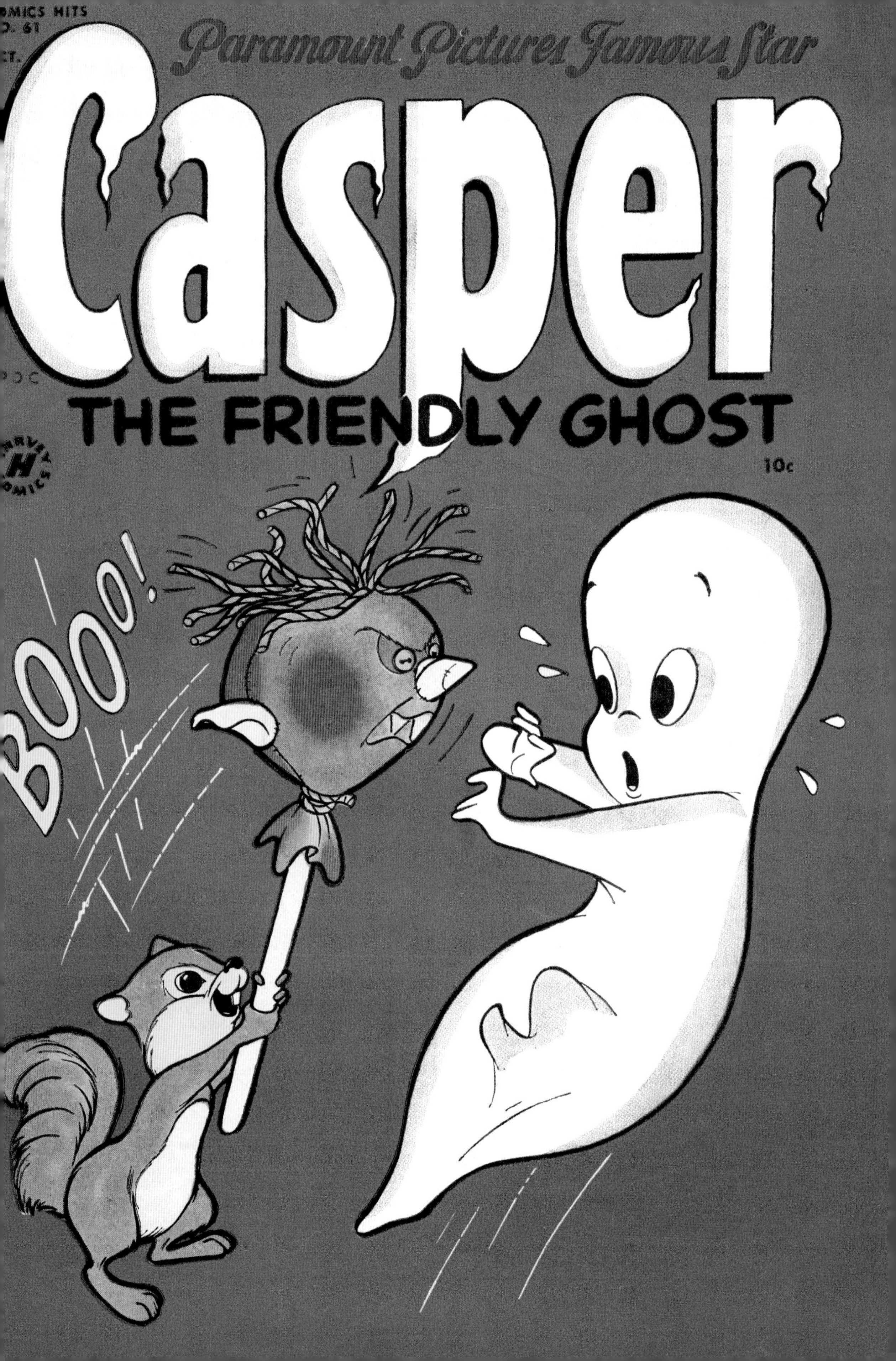

COMICS HITS
NO. 61
OCT.
Paramount Pictures Famous Star
Casper
THE FRIENDLY GHOST
10c
BOOO!

Amazing New Invention Makes Drawing Easy!

NOW YOU CAN EASILY DRAW PEOPLE, ANIMALS, OR STILL LIFE, OR MAPS LIKE AN ARTIST EVEN IF YOU HAVE NEVER DRAWN A STRAIGHT LINE BEFORE

DRAW INSTANTLY

NO EXPERIENCE
NO TALENT
NO LESSONS
NO SKILL NEEDED!

DRAW ANY TYPE OF DRAWING

Human figures, all objects, needlework, designs.
Dress designs, knitting, crocheting, etc.
Cartoons, comics, landscapes, buildings, etc.
Pictures, portraits, photographs, etc.
Still life, bowls, furniture, fruit, etc.
Copy maps, designs, decorations, blueprints for woodwork, machines, knitting, needlework, embroidery

This amazing new invention makes it easy for anyone to draw instantly!!

Now you can easily copy any picture and you can easily enlarge or reduce anything you wish to draw. Students get better school marks with it.

ONLY
$1.98
COMPLETE

Now, anyone from 5 to 90 can easily draw, paint, or sketch almost anything quickly and accurately the very first time you use the Master Art Helper. You draw like a professional artist even if you have never drawn before. Thousands who were told they were "hopeless" at drawing, now draw like professional artists, and draw those "tough" maps and paintings with ease! No matter what you want to draw with the use of the Master Art Helper, it is automatically seen on any sheet of paper, then you easily, quickly trace the picture on the paper because you already see it there—and in color too! It develops children's art ability and improves their drawing technique! With the Master Art Helper you will draw an accurate professional-type drawing that anyone would think an experienced artist had drawn. This often helps students to get better grades in school! The Master Art Helper makes it easy to draw or copy anything you wish to draw larger or smaller or any size you wish, and is excellent for drawing **MAPS** usually required of students. It can be used easily on any table, board, or desk anywhere, at home or in school. The Master Art Helper is used to draw photographs both in-doors and out-doors. It requires absolutely no lessons or practice. If you write with a pencil you can easily draw anything with the Master Art Helper. The Master Art Helper can help you be popular and can give you lots of hours of enjoyment.

HOW IT WORKS

Simply look through the Master Art Helper and see what you want to draw right on the paper you are using. All you do is trace the drawing—like magic you have drawn a perfect professional picture!

WIN POPULARITY! BE ADMIRED!

Your friends will ask you to draw them and you will easily be able to do it. The Master Art Helper will help make you popular. Thousands find that after a short time they can draw well without the Master Art Helper. It helps anyine to develop skills and artistic ability which often leads to a good paying career in art. Helps you draw window cards, maps, signs, portraits, living subjects, and used by many store keepers.

FREE!

"Easily Understood Tricks Of The Artist" This valuable booklet, "Easily Understood Tricks Of The Artist" will be included free with your Master Art Helper. This booklet will help you understand many of the techniques of the proper shading and proportion and so forth, that are used in drawing human figures and maps. And, will help you improve your drawing skill.

MONEY BACK GUARANTEE. 10 DAY FREE TRIAL

If the Master Art Helper doesn't help you to draw anything you want to draw. If you can't draw people, animals, maps, figures, or anything else like a professional artist with this Master Art Helper, return it within 10 days and your money will be refunded.

STANDARD MODEL

$1.98

MASTER ART HELPER COMPANY
318 MARKET STREET DEPT. 18, NEWARK, NEW JERSEY

10 Day Free Trial! Mail Coupon Now!

MASTER ART HELPER CO. Dept. 18
318 Market Street
Newark, New Jersey

Rush me the Master Art Helper and your free booklet, "Easily Understood Tricks Of The Artist"
I enclose $1.98 send postage prepaid
I understand I can return this merchandise after a 10 day trial and my money will be refunded.
I enclose $2.98 send Deluxe Model.

Name..

Address..

City........................ Zone........ State........................

SENT ON APPROVAL
Excellent for drawing required in school, office, shop, or store.

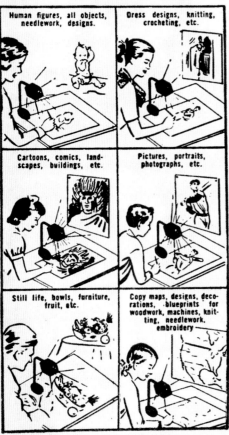

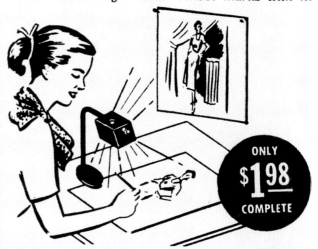

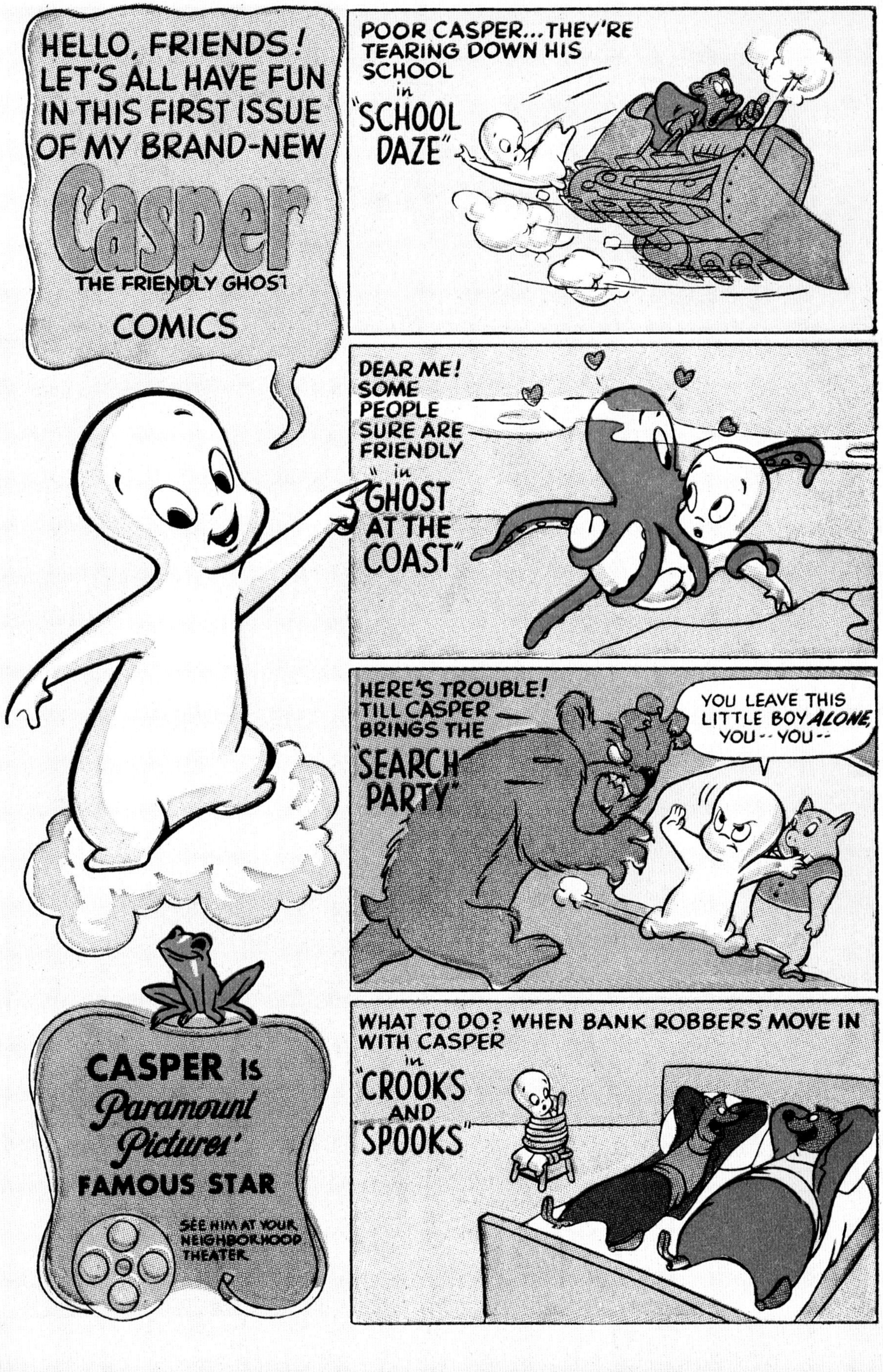

HELLO, FRIENDS! LET'S ALL HAVE FUN IN THIS FIRST ISSUE OF MY BRAND-NEW
Casper
THE FRIENDLY GHOST
COMICS
POOR CASPER... THEY'RE TEARING DOWN HIS SCHOOL in "SCHOOL DAZE"
DEAR ME! SOME PEOPLE SURE ARE FRIENDLY in "GHOST AT THE COAST"
HERE'S TROUBLE! TILL CASPER BRINGS THE "SEARCH PARTY"
YOU LEAVE THIS LITTLE BOY ALONE, YOU -- YOU --
CASPER IS Paramount Pictures' FAMOUS STAR
SEE HIM AT YOUR NEIGHBORHOOD THEATER
WHAT TO DO? WHEN BANK ROBBERS MOVE IN WITH CASPER in "CROOKS AND SPOOKS"

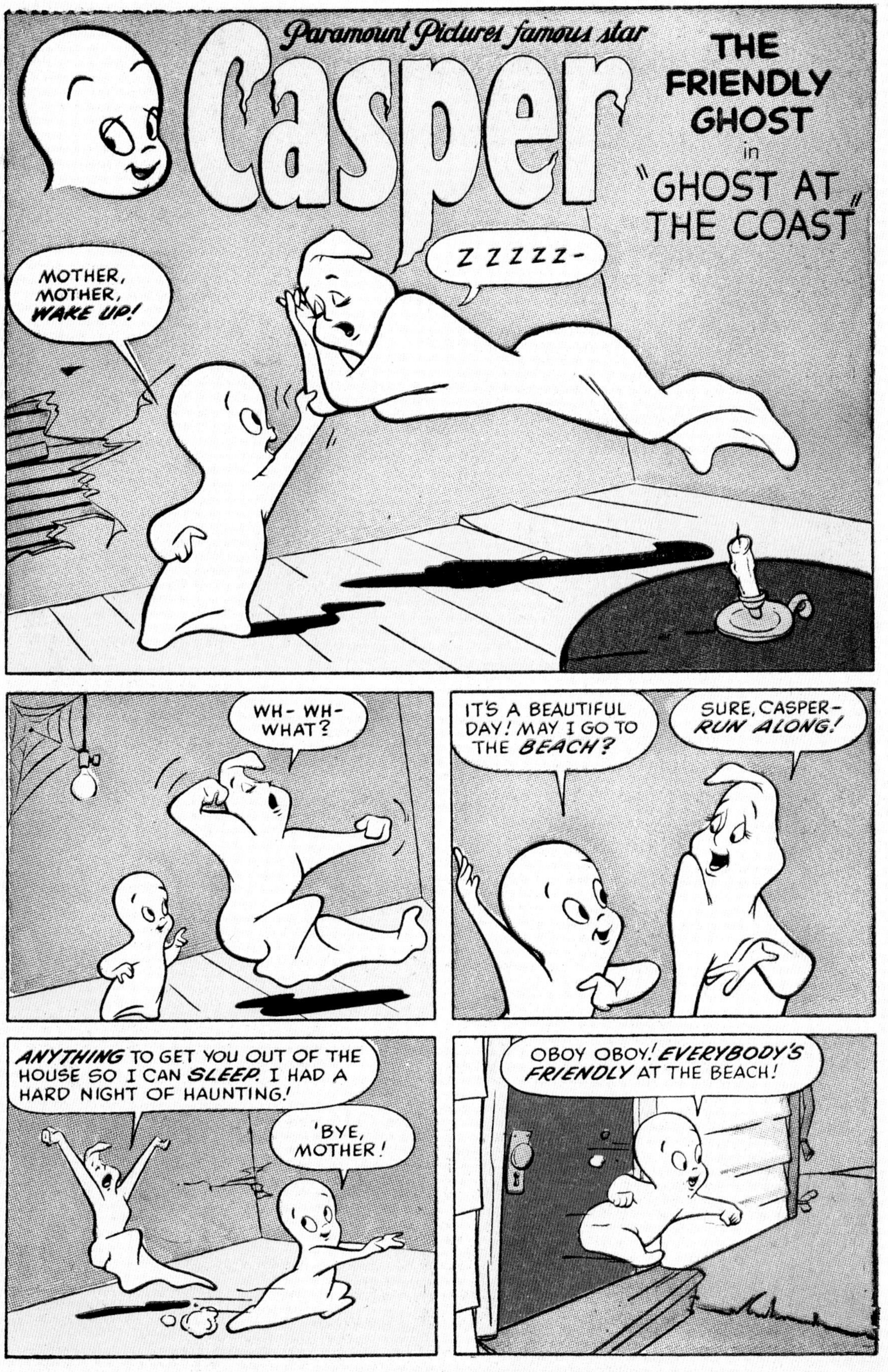
Paramount Pictures famous star
Casper
THE FRIENDLY GHOST
in
"GHOST AT THE COAST"
MOTHER, MOTHER, WAKE UP!
Z Z Z Z Z -
WH- WH- WHAT?
IT'S A BEAUTIFUL DAY! MAY I GO TO THE BEACH?
SURE, CASPER- RUN ALONG!
ANYTHING TO GET YOU OUT OF THE HOUSE SO I CAN SLEEP. I HAD A HARD NIGHT OF HAUNTING!
'BYE, MOTHER!
OBOY OBOY! EVERYBODY'S FRIENDLY AT THE BEACH!

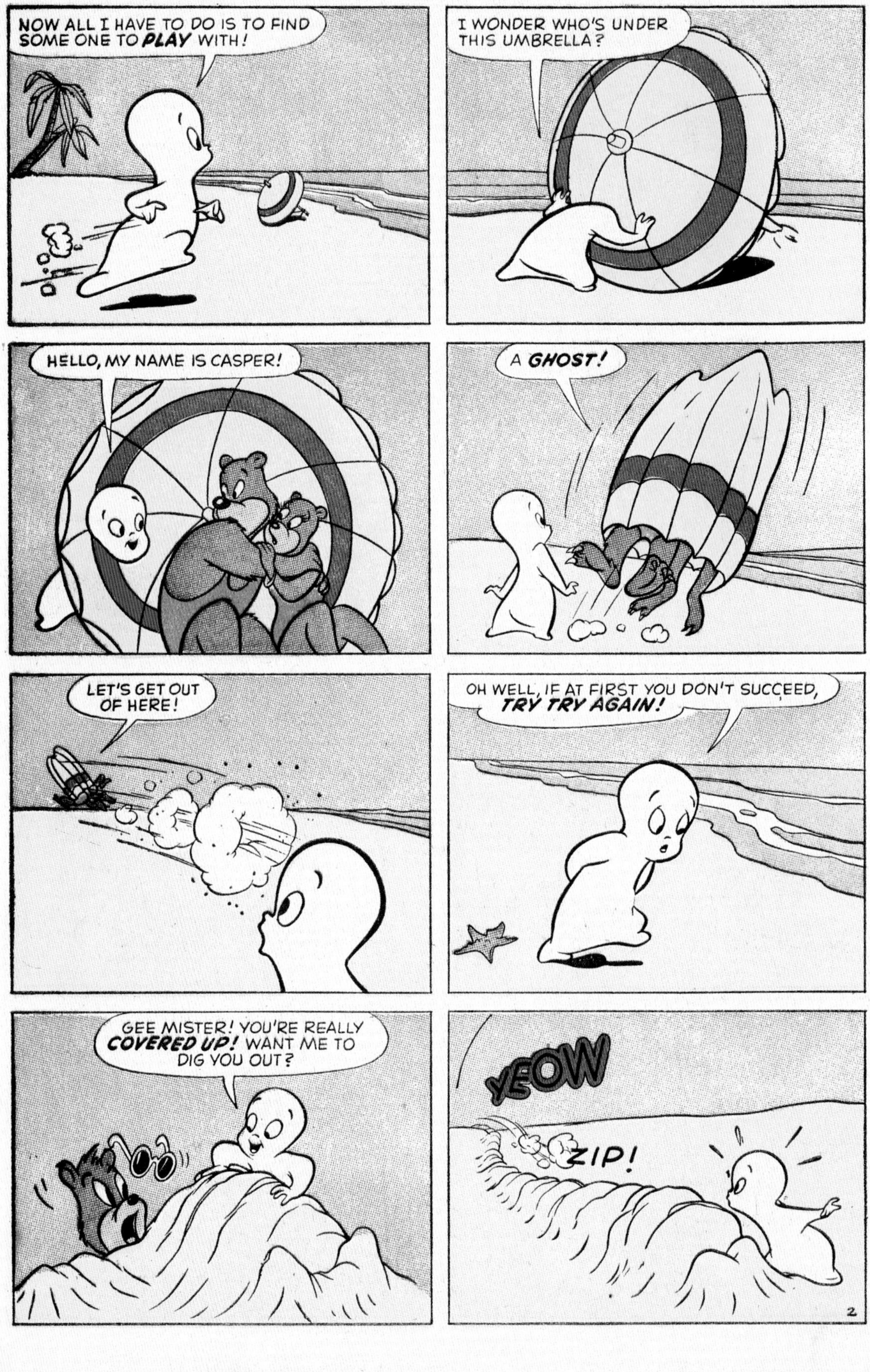
NOW ALL I HAVE TO DO IS TO FIND SOME ONE TO PLAY WITH!
I WONDER WHO'S UNDER THIS UMBRELLA?
HELLO, MY NAME IS CASPER!
A GHOST!
LET'S GET OUT OF HERE!
OH WELL, IF AT FIRST YOU DON'T SUCCEED, TRY TRY AGAIN!
GEE MISTER! YOU'RE REALLY COVERED UP! WANT ME TO DIG YOU OUT?
YEOW
ZIP!

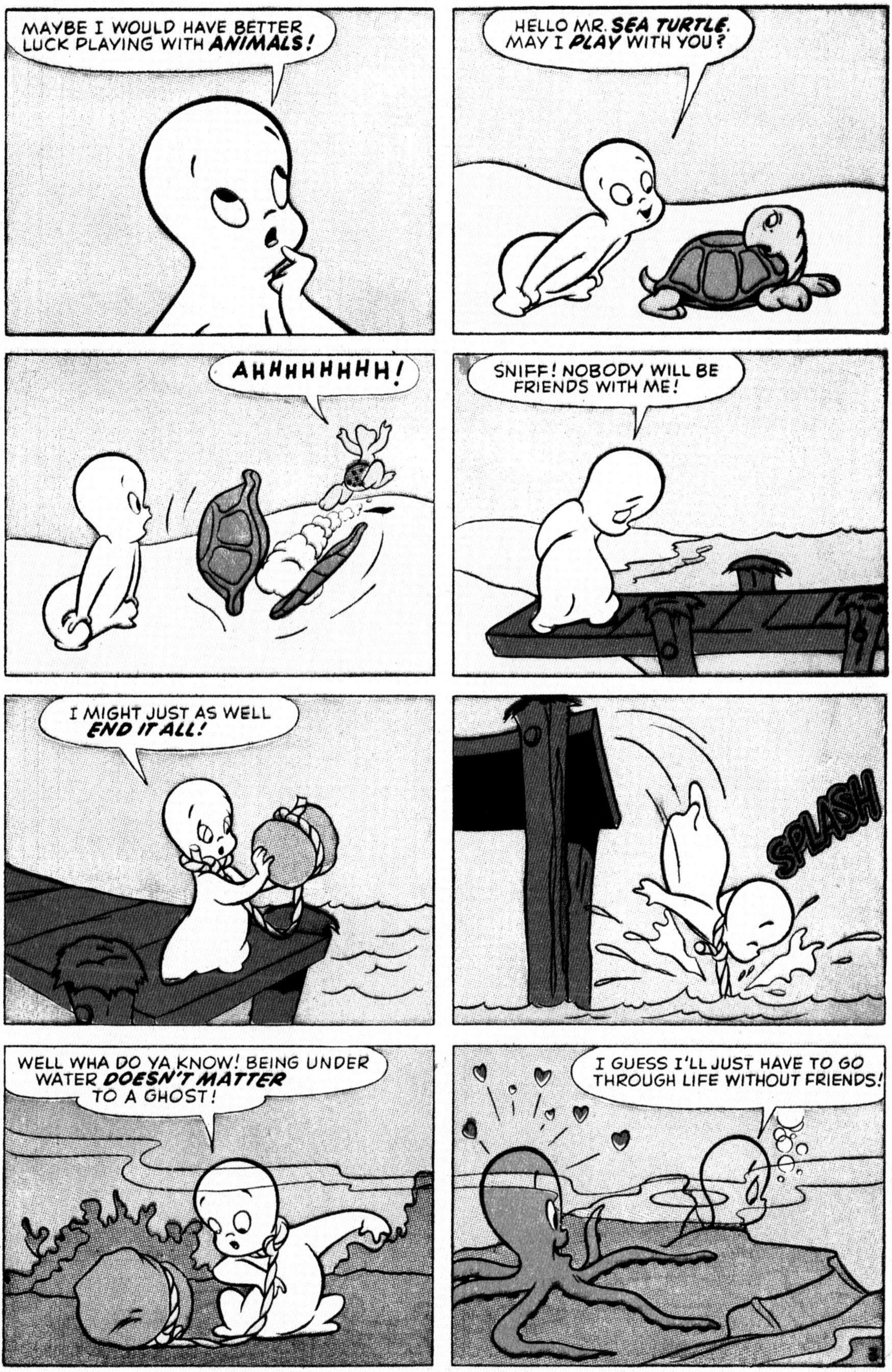
MAYBE I WOULD HAVE BETTER LUCK PLAYING WITH ANIMALS!
HELLO MR. SEA TURTLE. MAY I PLAY WITH YOU?
AHHHHHHHH!
SNIFF! NOBODY WILL BE FRIENDS WITH ME!
I MIGHT JUST AS WELL END IT ALL!
SPLASH
WELL WHA DO YA KNOW! BEING UNDER WATER DOESN'T MATTER TO A GHOST!
I GUESS I'LL JUST HAVE TO GO THROUGH LIFE WITHOUT FRIENDS!

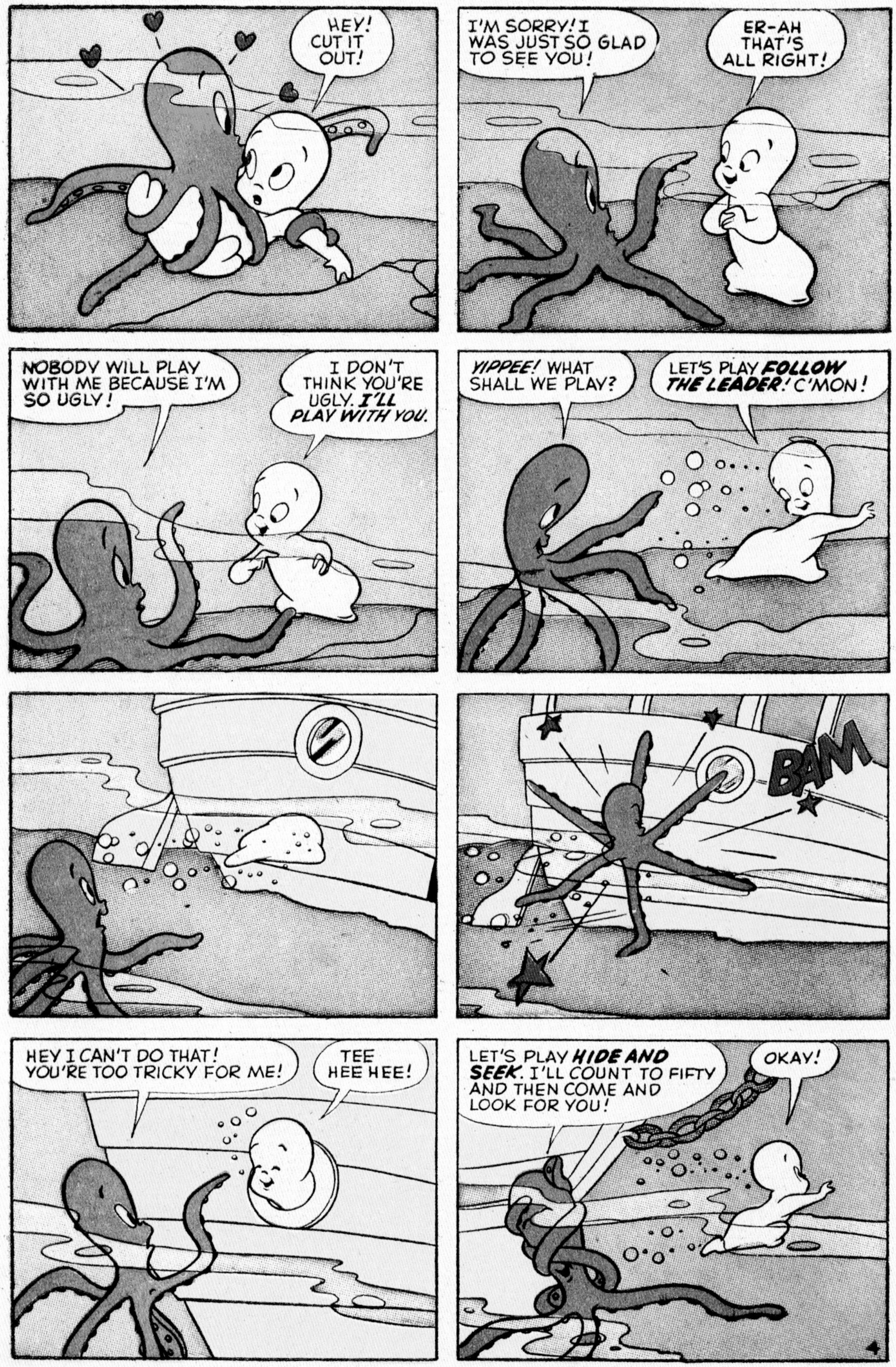
HEY! CUT IT OUT!
I'M SORRY! I WAS JUST SO GLAD TO SEE YOU!
ER-AH THAT'S ALL RIGHT!
NOBODY WILL PLAY WITH ME BECAUSE I'M SO UGLY!
I DON'T THINK YOU'RE UGLY. I'LL PLAY WITH YOU.
YIPPEE! WHAT SHALL WE PLAY?
LET'S PLAY FOLLOW THE LEADER! C'MON!
BAM
HEY I CAN'T DO THAT! YOU'RE TOO TRICKY FOR ME!
TEE HEE HEE!
LET'S PLAY HIDE AND SEEK. I'LL COUNT TO FIFTY AND THEN COME AND LOOK FOR YOU!
OKAY!
4

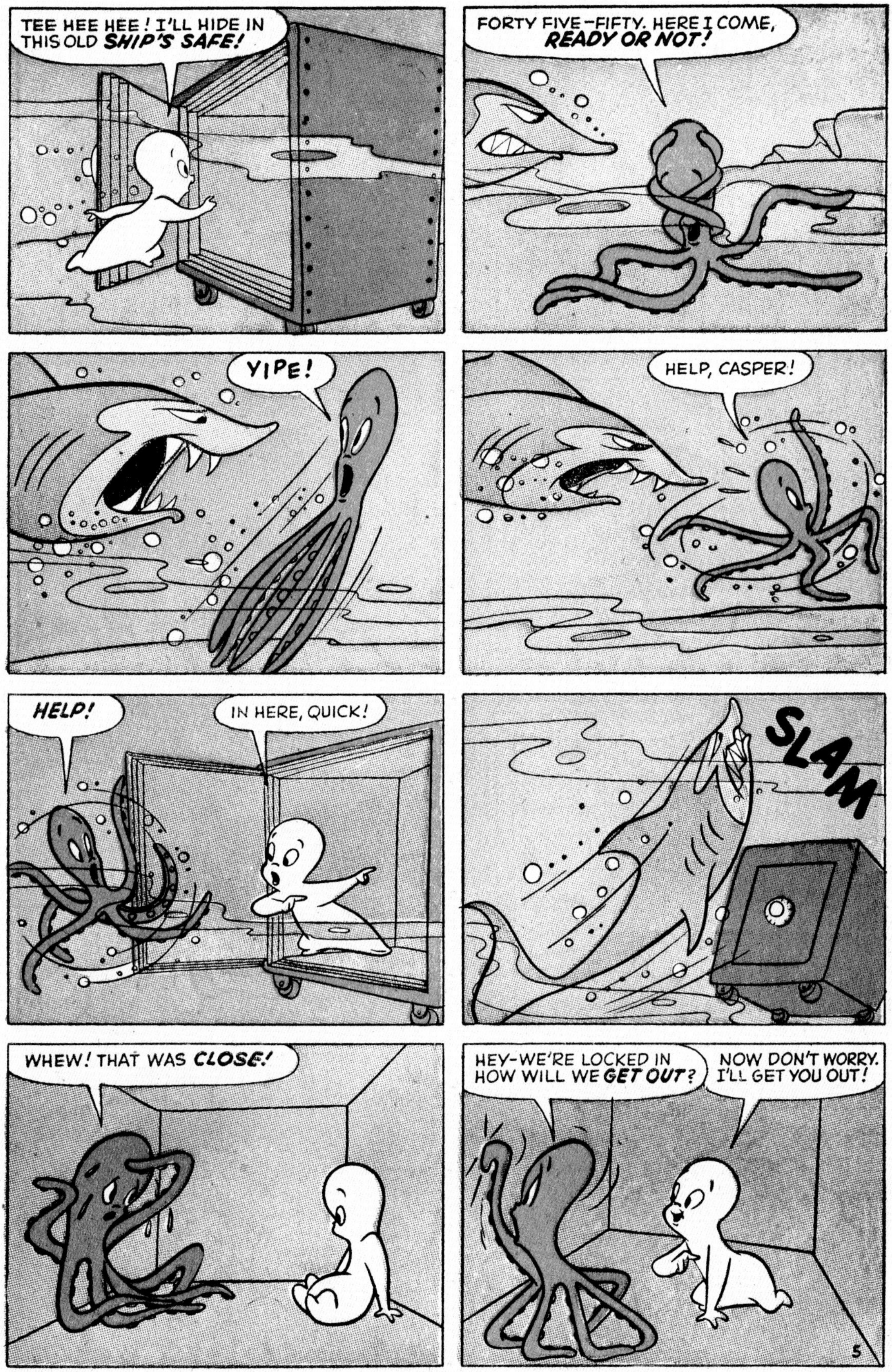
TEE HEE HEE! I'LL HIDE IN THIS OLD SHIP'S SAFE!
FORTY FIVE-FIFTY. HERE I COME, READY OR NOT!
YIPE!
HELP, CASPER!
HELP!
IN HERE, QUICK!
SLAM
WHEW! THAT WAS CLOSE!
HEY-WE'RE LOCKED IN HOW WILL WE GET OUT?
NOW DON'T WORRY. I'LL GET YOU OUT!

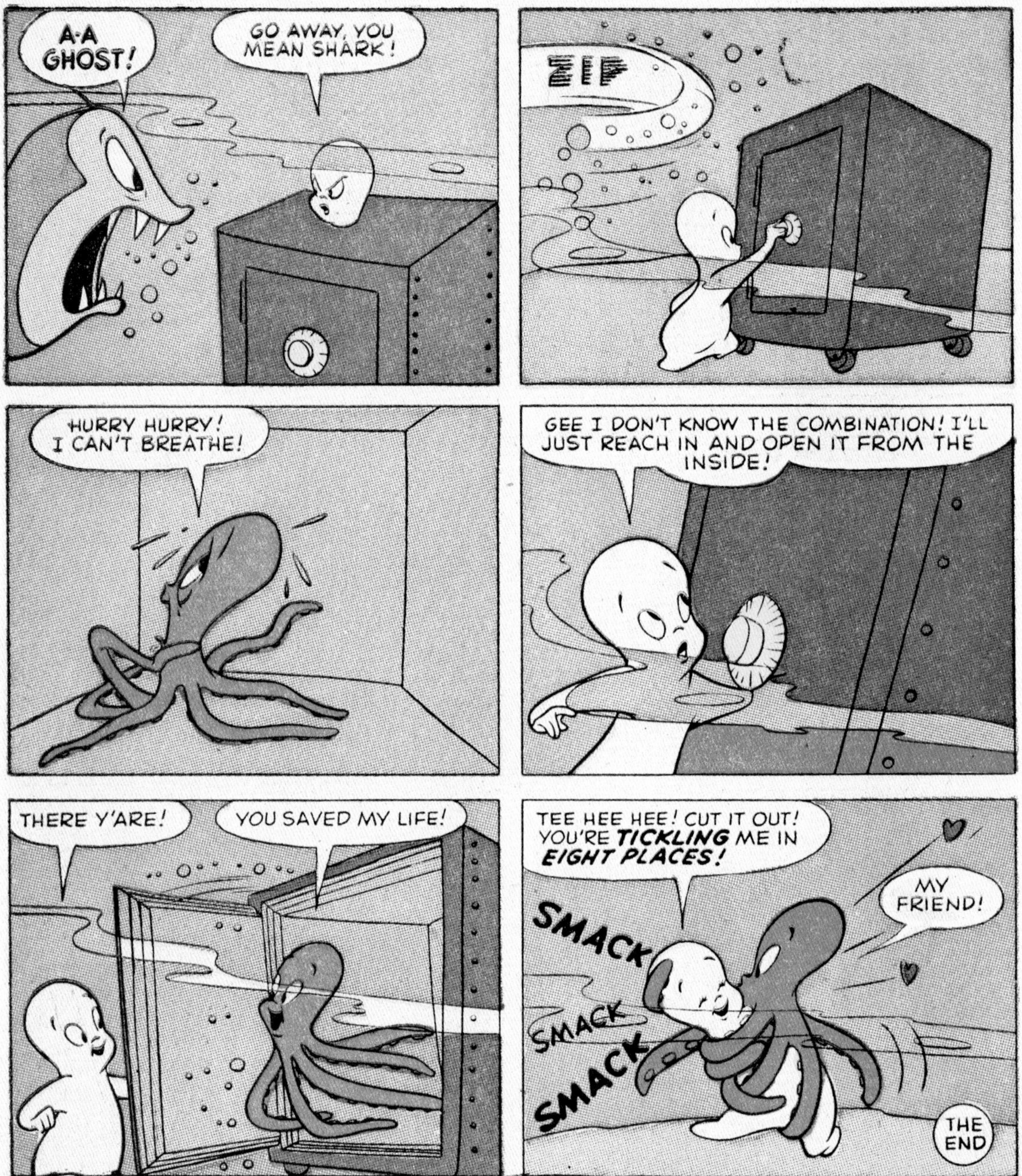
A-A GHOST!
GO AWAY, YOU MEAN SHARK!
ZIP
HURRY HURRY! I CAN'T BREATHE!
GEE I DON'T KNOW THE COMBINATION! I'LL JUST REACH IN AND OPEN IT FROM THE INSIDE!
THERE Y'ARE!
YOU SAVED MY LIFE!
TEE HEE HEE! CUT IT OUT! YOU'RE **TICKLING** ME IN ***EIGHT PLACES!***
MY FRIEND!
SMACK
SMACK
SMACK
THE END

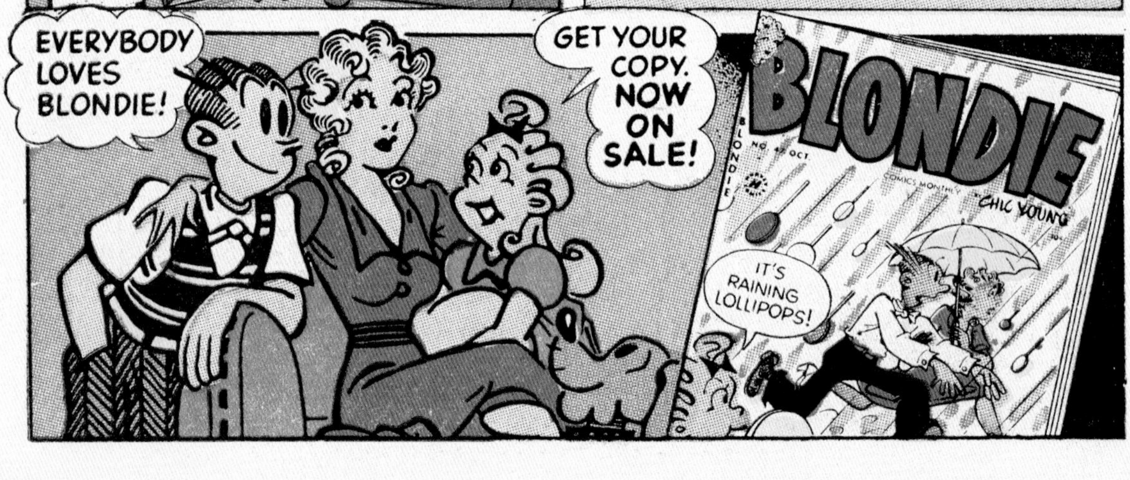
EVERYBODY LOVES BLONDIE!
GET YOUR COPY. NOW ON SALE!
BLONDIE
CHIC YOUNG
IT'S RAINING LOLLIPOPS!

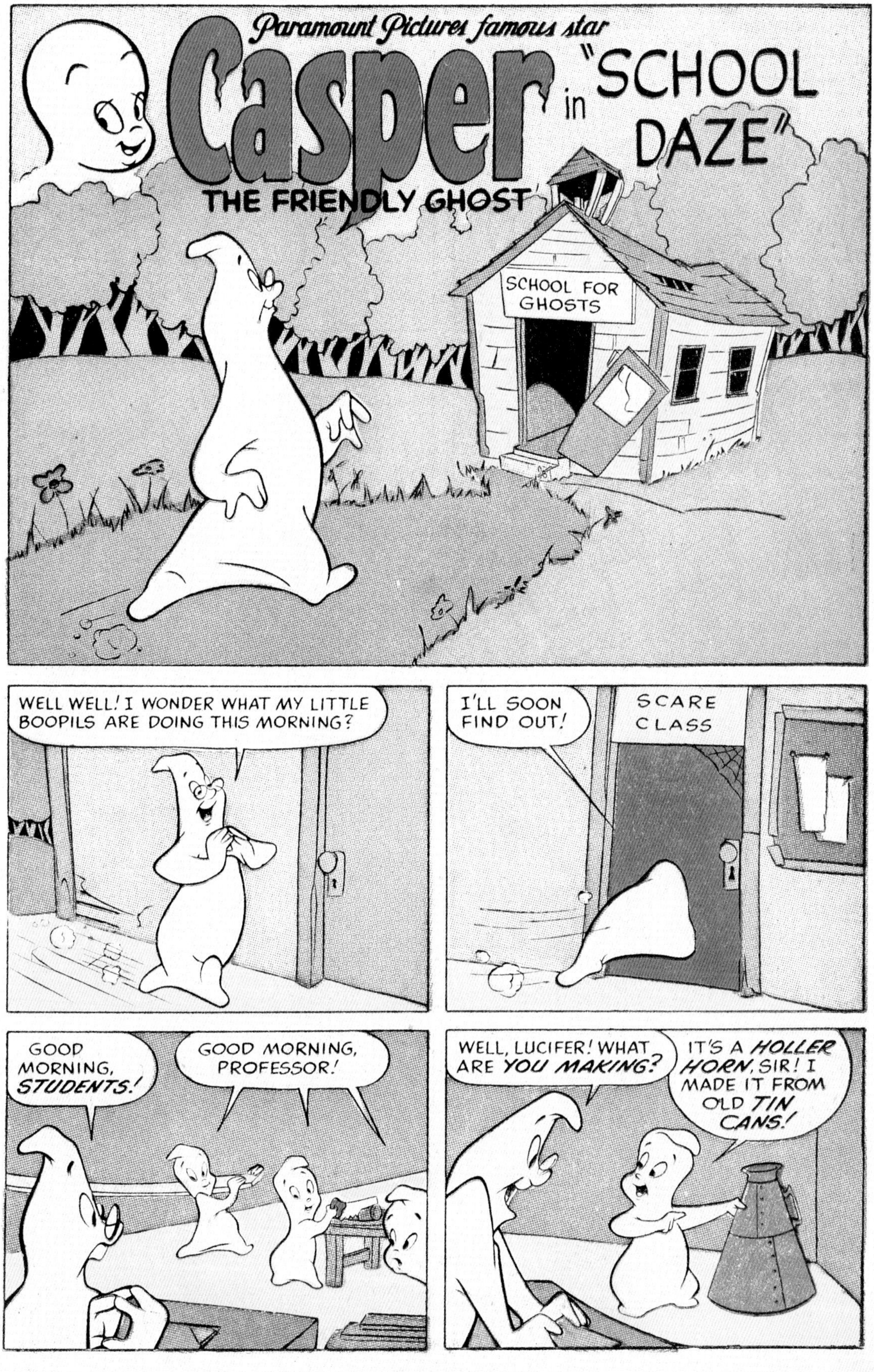
Paramount Pictures famous star
Casper
THE FRIENDLY GHOST
in "SCHOOL DAZE"
SCHOOL FOR GHOSTS
WELL WELL! I WONDER WHAT MY LITTLE BOOPILS ARE DOING THIS MORNING?
I'LL SOON FIND OUT!
SCARE CLASS
GOOD MORNING, STUDENTS!
GOOD MORNING, PROFESSOR!
WELL, LUCIFER! WHAT ARE YOU MAKING?
IT'S A HOLLER HORN, SIR! I MADE IT FROM OLD TIN CANS!

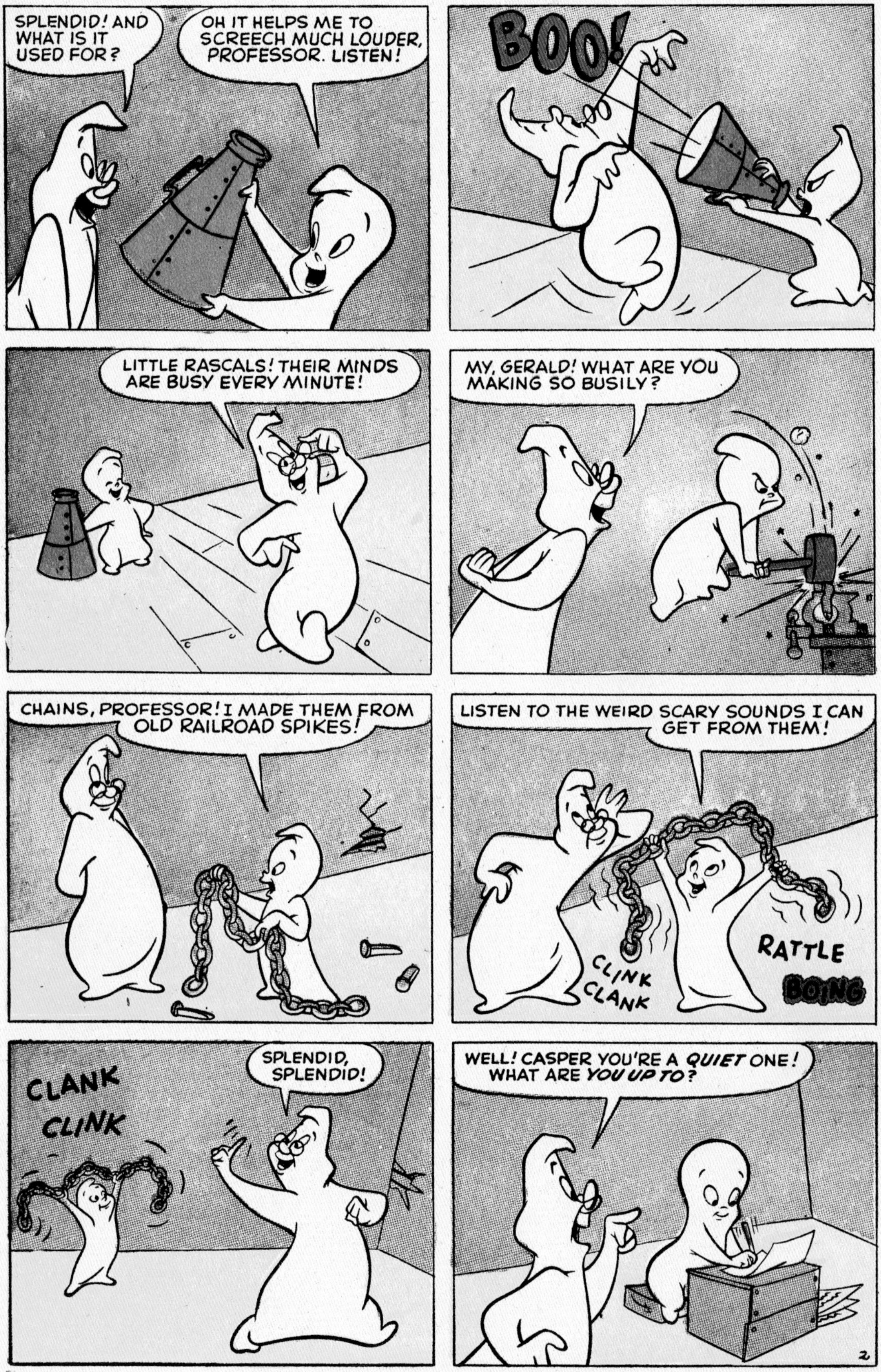

SPLENDID! AND WHAT IS IT USED FOR?
OH IT HELPS ME TO SCREECH MUCH LOUDER, PROFESSOR. LISTEN!
BOO!
LITTLE RASCALS! THEIR MINDS ARE BUSY EVERY MINUTE!
MY, GERALD! WHAT ARE YOU MAKING SO BUSILY?
CHAINS, PROFESSOR! I MADE THEM FROM OLD RAILROAD SPIKES!
LISTEN TO THE WEIRD SCARY SOUNDS I CAN GET FROM THEM!
CLINK
CLANK
RATTLE
BOING
CLANK
CLINK
SPLENDID, SPLENDID!
WELL! CASPER YOU'RE A *QUIET* ONE! WHAT ARE *YOU UP TO*?

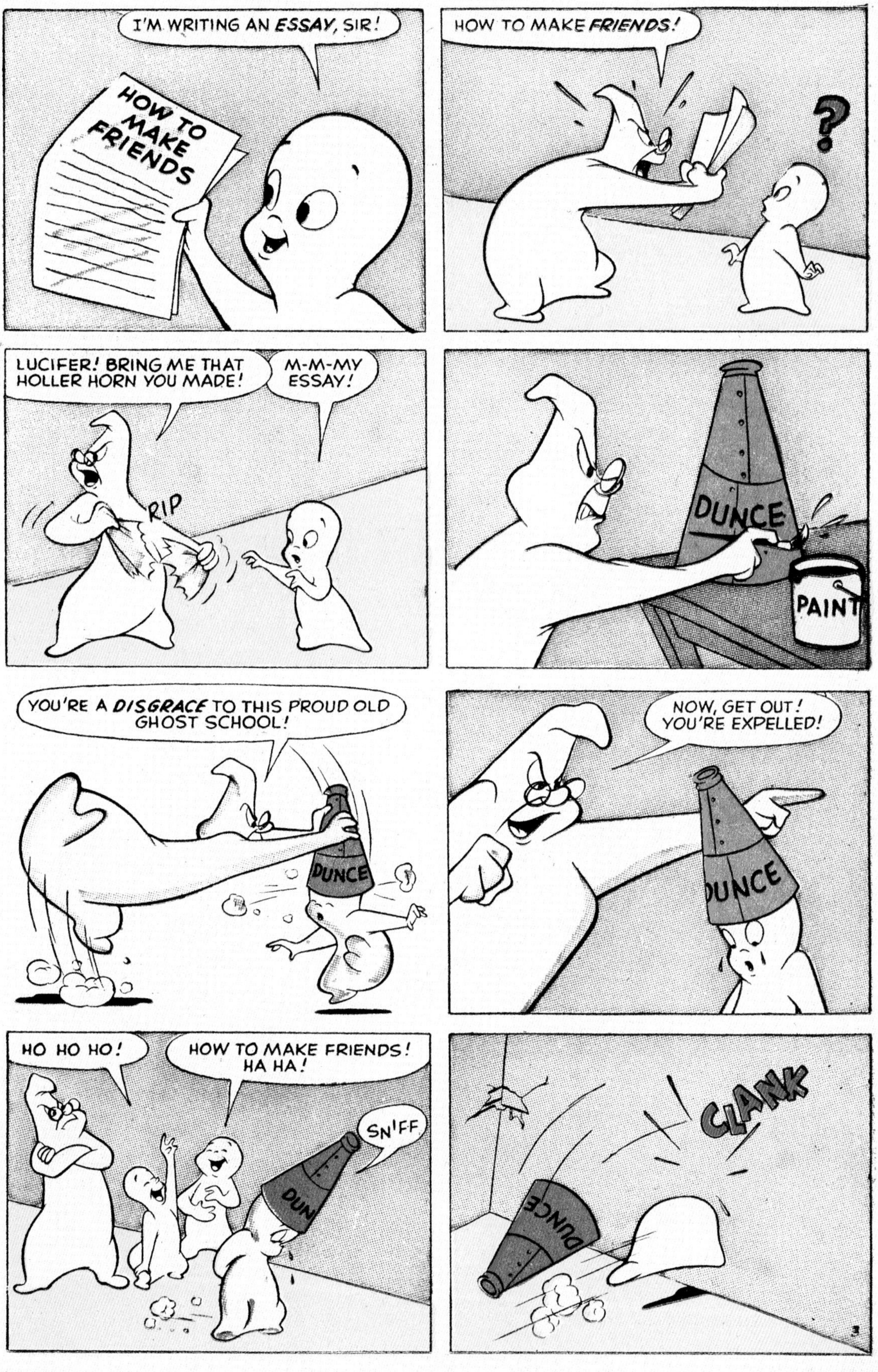
I'M WRITING AN ESSAY, SIR!
HOW TO MAKE FRIENDS
HOW TO MAKE FRIENDS!
?
LUCIFER! BRING ME THAT HOLLER HORN YOU MADE!
M-M-MY ESSAY!
RIP
DUNCE
PAINT
YOU'RE A DISGRACE TO THIS PROUD OLD GHOST SCHOOL!
DUNCE
NOW, GET OUT! YOU'RE EXPELLED!
DUNCE
HO HO HO!
HOW TO MAKE FRIENDS! HA HA!
SNIFF
DUN
CLANK
DUNCE

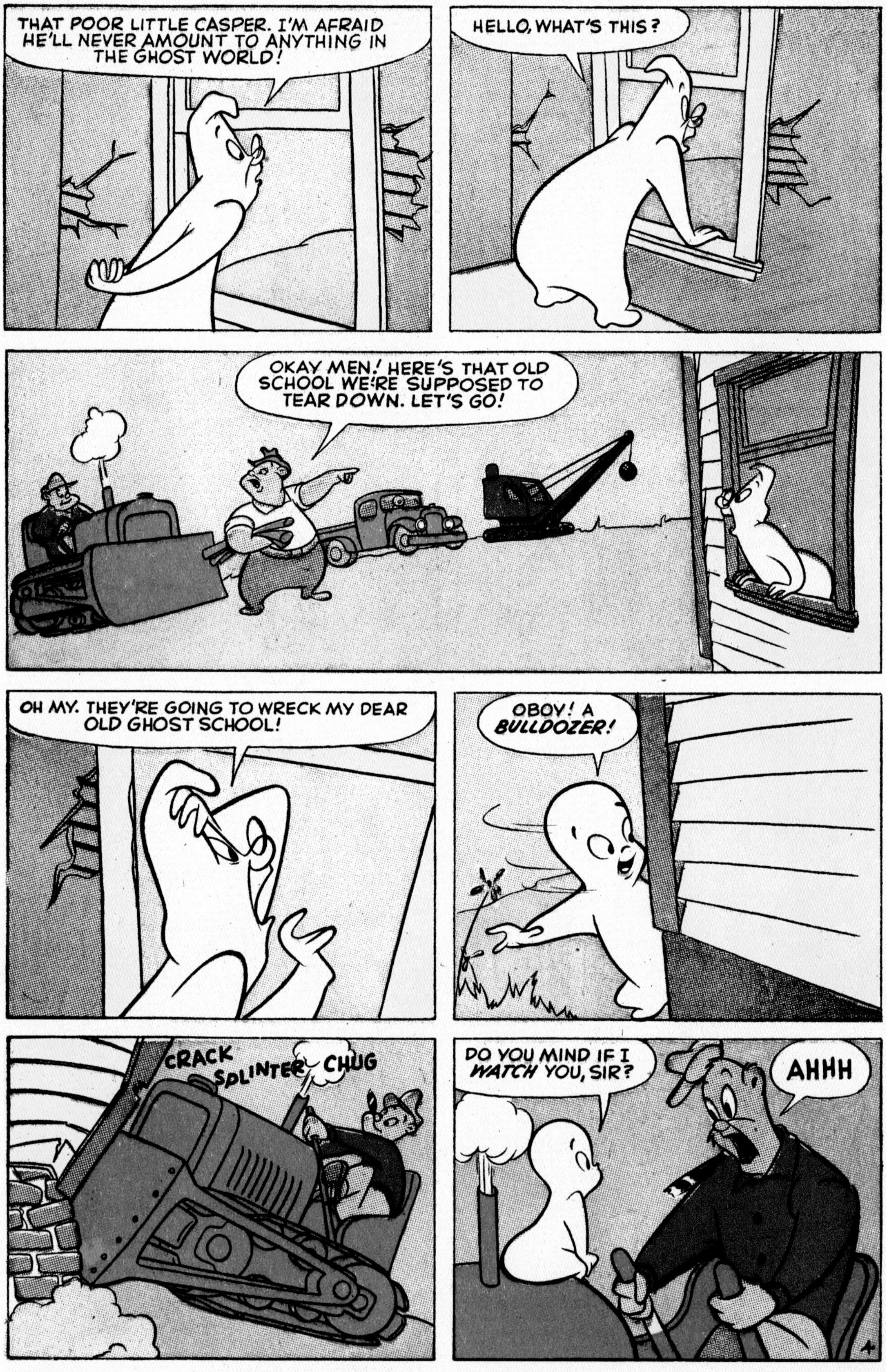
THAT POOR LITTLE CASPER. I'M AFRAID HE'LL NEVER AMOUNT TO ANYTHING IN THE GHOST WORLD!
HELLO, WHAT'S THIS?
OKAY MEN! HERE'S THAT OLD SCHOOL WE'RE SUPPOSED TO TEAR DOWN. LET'S GO!
OH MY. THEY'RE GOING TO WRECK MY DEAR OLD GHOST SCHOOL!
OBOY! A BULLDOZER!
CRACK
SPLINTER
CHUG
DO YOU MIND IF I WATCH YOU, SIR?
AHHH
4

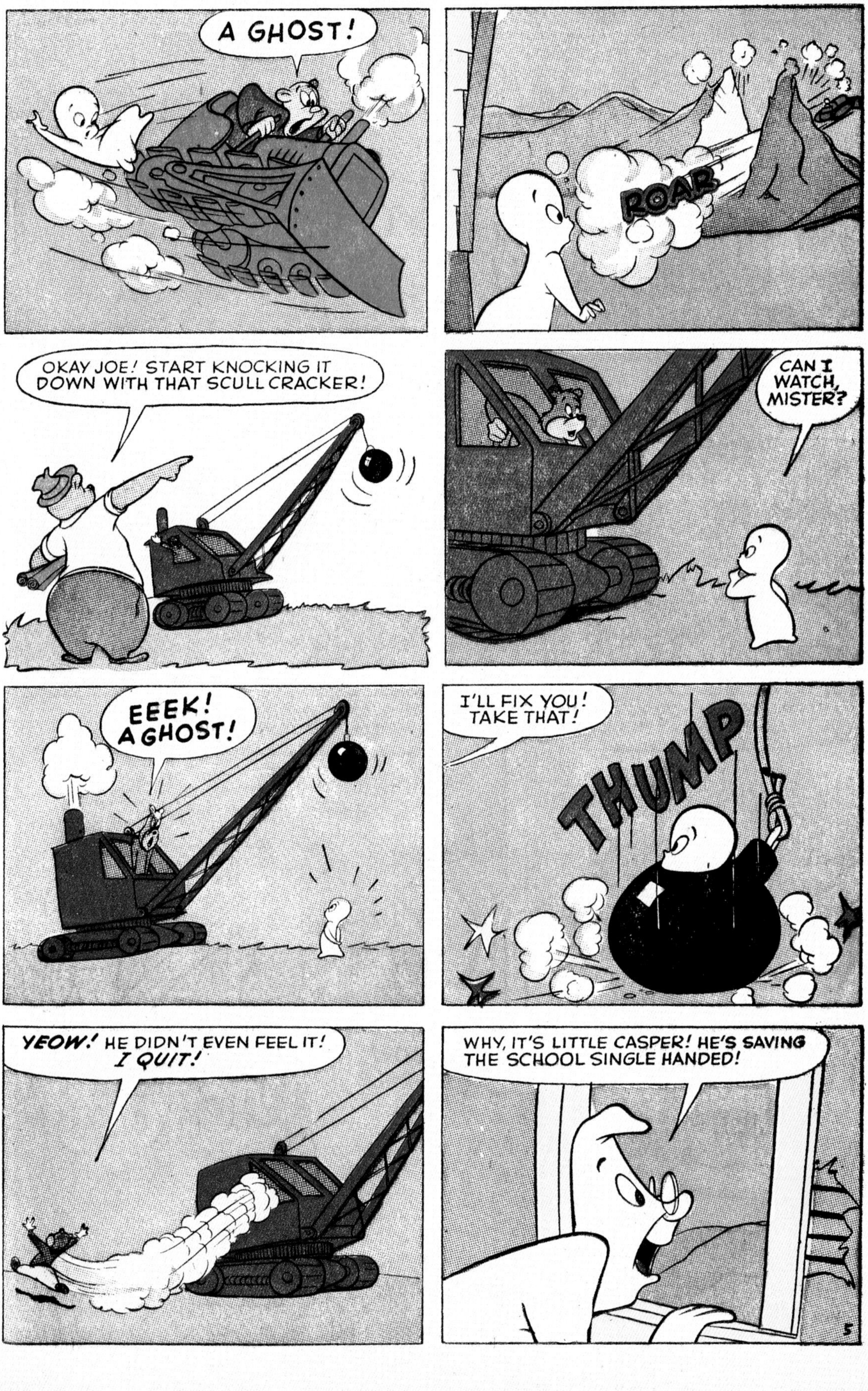

A GHOST!
ROAR
OKAY JOE! START KNOCKING IT DOWN WITH THAT SCULL CRACKER!
CAN I WATCH, MISTER?
EEEK! A GHOST!
I'LL FIX YOU! TAKE THAT!
THUMP
YEOW! HE DIDN'T EVEN FEEL IT! I QUIT!
WHY, IT'S LITTLE CASPER! HE'S SAVING THE SCHOOL SINGLE HANDED!

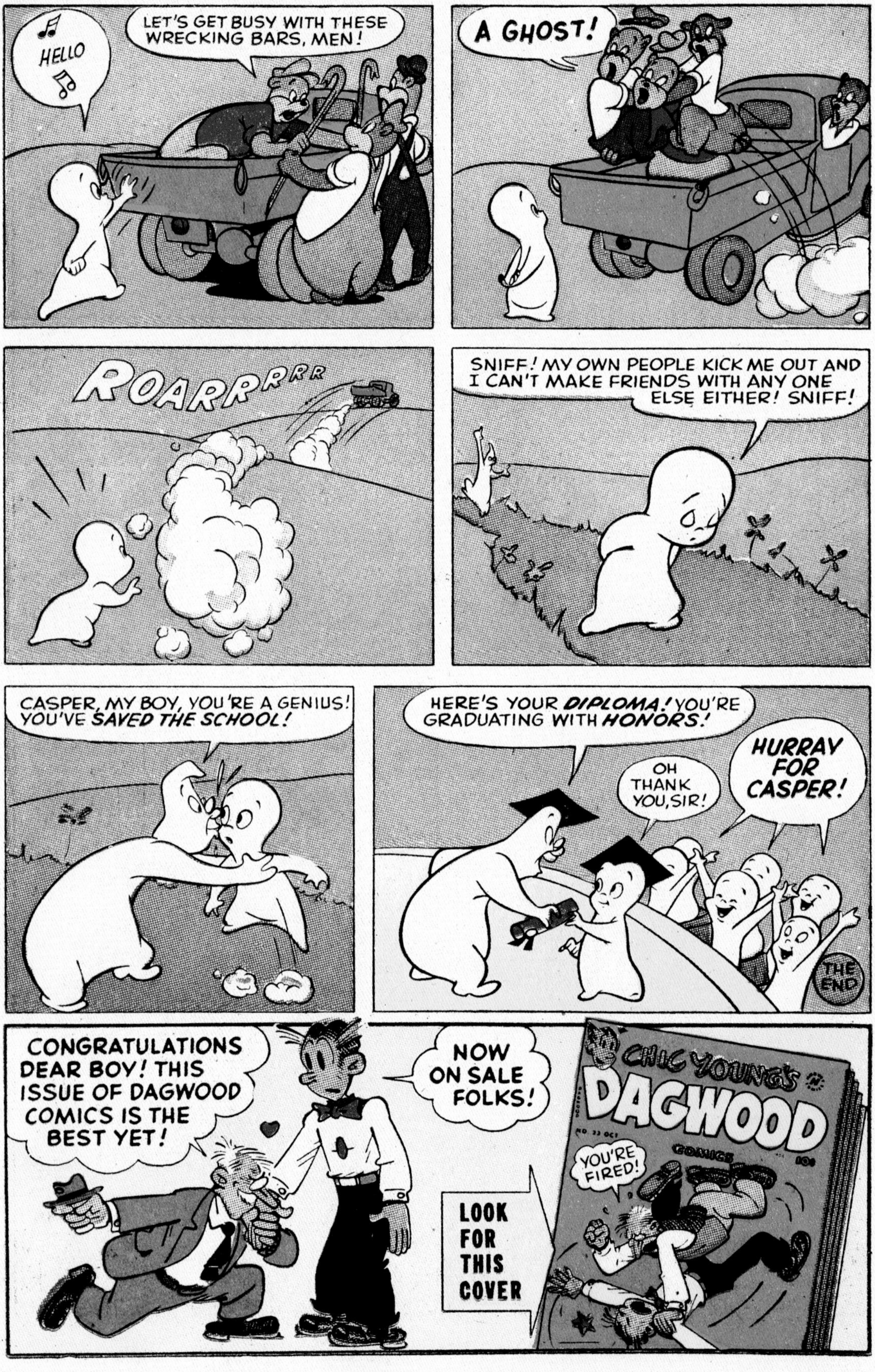
HELLO
LET'S GET BUSY WITH THESE WRECKING BARS, MEN!
A GHOST!
ROARRRRRR
SNIFF! MY OWN PEOPLE KICK ME OUT AND I CAN'T MAKE FRIENDS WITH ANY ONE ELSE EITHER! SNIFF!
CASPER, MY BOY, YOU'RE A GENIUS! YOU'VE SAVED THE SCHOOL!
HERE'S YOUR DIPLOMA! YOU'RE GRADUATING WITH HONORS!
OH THANK YOU, SIR!
HURRAY FOR CASPER!
THE END
CONGRATULATIONS DEAR BOY! THIS ISSUE OF DAGWOOD COMICS IS THE BEST YET!
NOW ON SALE FOLKS!
LOOK FOR THIS COVER
CHIC YOUNG'S
DAGWOOD
COMICS
YOU'RE FIRED!

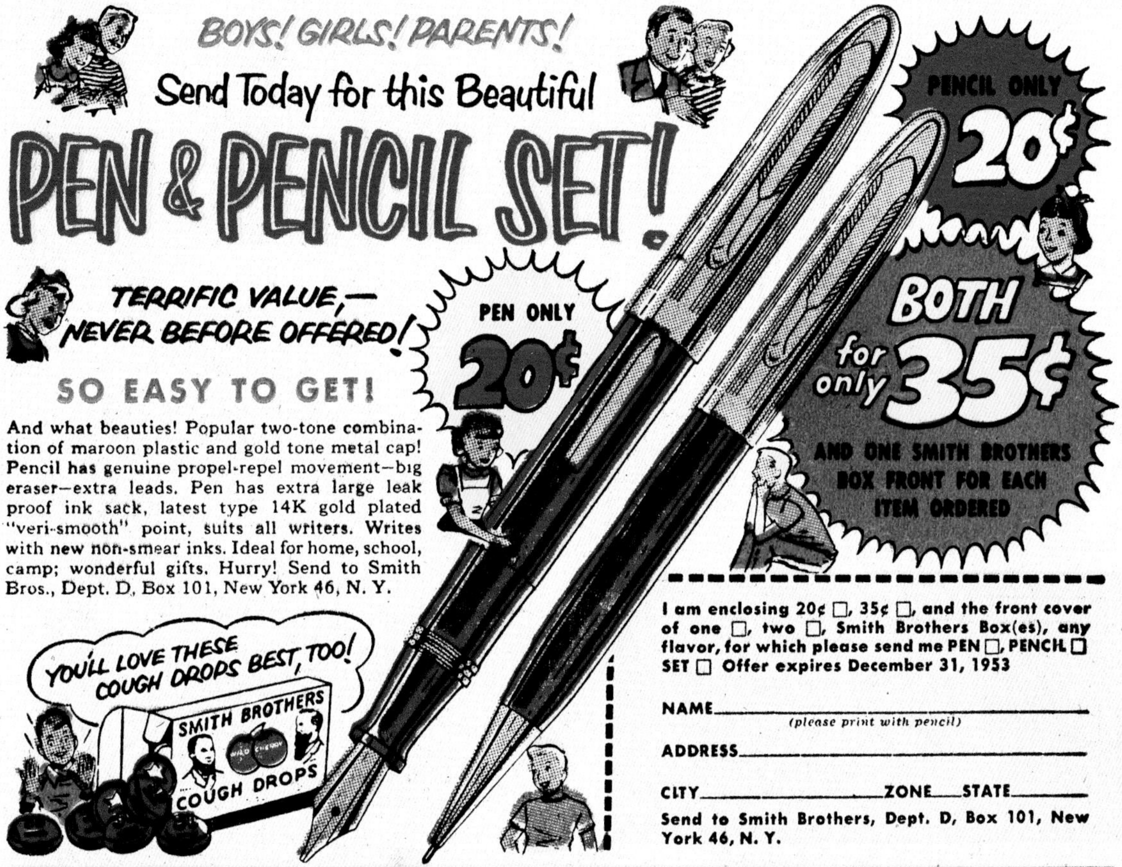
BOYS! GIRLS! PARENTS!
Send Today for this Beautiful
PEN & PENCIL SET!
TERRIFIC VALUE,— NEVER BEFORE OFFERED!
SO EASY TO GET!
And what beauties! Popular two-tone combination of maroon plastic and gold tone metal cap! Pencil has genuine propel-repel movement—big eraser—extra leads. Pen has extra large leak proof ink sack, latest type 14K gold plated "veri-smooth" point, suits all writers. Writes with new non-smear inks. Ideal for home, school, camp; wonderful gifts. Hurry! Send to Smith Bros., Dept. D, Box 101, New York 46, N. Y.
PEN ONLY 20¢
PENCIL ONLY 20¢
BOTH for only 35¢
AND ONE SMITH BROTHERS BOX FRONT FOR EACH ITEM ORDERED
YOU'LL LOVE THESE COUGH DROPS BEST, TOO!
SMITH BROTHERS
COUGH DROPS
I am enclosing 20¢ ☐, 35¢ ☐, and the front cover of one ☐, two ☐, Smith Brothers Box(es), any flavor, for which please send me PEN ☐, PENCIL ☐ SET ☐ Offer expires December 31, 1953
NAME
(please print with pencil)
ADDRESS
CITY ZONE STATE
Send to Smith Brothers, Dept. D, Box 101, New York 46, N. Y.

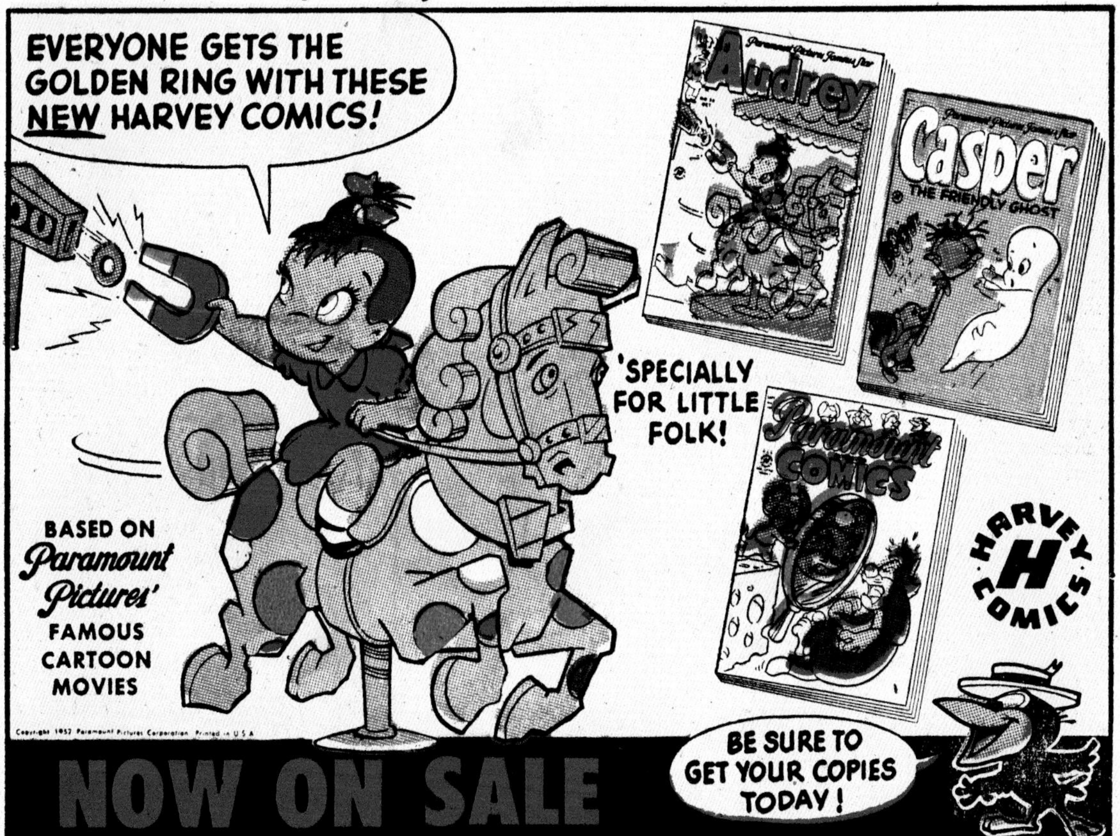
EVERYONE GETS THE GOLDEN RING WITH THESE NEW HARVEY COMICS!
Audrey
Casper THE FRIENDLY GHOST
'SPECIALLY FOR LITTLE FOLK!
Paramount COMICS
BASED ON Paramount Pictures' FAMOUS CARTOON MOVIES
HARVEY H COMICS
Copyright 1952 Paramount Pictures Corporation Printed in U S A
NOW ON SALE
BE SURE TO GET YOUR COPIES TODAY!

CASPER'S FRIENDS (HE'S VERY FRIENDLY)

CASPER'S PICTURE ALBUM

BABY ANIMALS LIKE CASPER

BUT FRIENDLY CASPER WANTS *EVERYBODY* TO BE HIS FRIEND.

CASPER HAS LOTS OF SMALL CHILDREN FRIENDS

BIRDS LOVE CASPER

OH, YES! YOU'RE CASPER'S FRIEND, TOO!

WHERE CASPER LIVES (HE HAS MANY HOMES)

SOMETIMES CASPER LIVES IN OLD CASTLES

SOMETIMES HE LIVES BEHIND AN OLD TOMBSTONE..

CASPER HAS EVEN LIVED WITH BATS IN A BELFRY

PLACES CASPER HAS VISITED

CASPER HAS BEEN UNDER THE OCEAN

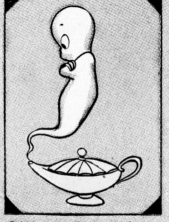

ONCE CASPER CAME OUT OF ALADDIN'S LAMP!

CASPER MADE FRIENDS WITH MOTHER GOOSE WHEN HE WENT TO MOTHER GOOSE LAND

BEST FIRE ENGINE

"I'm tired of fires!" sobbed Chester passionately. "I'm tired of racing my wheels off to get there on time! I'm tired of being pulled out of bed at all hours of the night, interrupted at all hours of the day! I'm tired of the smoke and the noise and the heat! *I'm just plain sick and tired of it all!* I'll never go to another fire again!!"

"WHAT?" roared the deep bass voice of Zachariah, the oldest engine in the yard "Why, what's a fire engine *for*, if not to go to fires?? Of all the . . ."

CLANG! CLANG! CLANG! The sudden blasting of the fire alarm interrupted him. In two seconds the whole yard was a beehive of activity! Zachariah's voice rose above the din. "Come along just this once, Chester!" he shouted. "And stick close behind me all the way!"

"But I oh, all right! But this is absolutely, positively, the *last time*!" Chester shouted back. "And it's only because I don't want to be disrespectful . . ."

But Zachariah was already half-way out of the yard. Chester had no choice but to follow—and follow he did, right up to the blazing building itself!

"Now!" commanded Zachariah sternly. "Look around you, boy! Look at that little baby over there!" He pointed to a tiny infant nestled in his mother's arms. A fireman—one of Chester's crew, in fact—was leading mother and child to safety. "If you hadn't brought that fireman here," continued Zachariah, "that infant, and its mother, would have been trapped in the fire! Now look up there . . ." He pointed to a high window from which poured smoke and flames. A squad of firemen balanced a ladder up to the window, and one by one, the people inside the burning room were climbing down to safety. "If you hadn't carried that ladder, all those people would have been trapped, too!" observed Zachariah. "Now look over there . . ." He pointed to the building next door which was being showered with sparks from the fire. The firemen played their hoses all over it to keep the blaze from spreading. "If you hadn't carried that hose over here, that building would catch on fire, too, and a million dollars worth of property would have been damaged . . ."

"Stop! Stop!" sobbed Chester. "I've been a selfish, spoiled brat! I never stopped to think . . ." He couldn't go on. He was crying too hard!

"There! There!" The oldest engine's voice was gentle. "We all make mistakes! I'll bet you'll be the best fire engine in the whole yard from now on!"

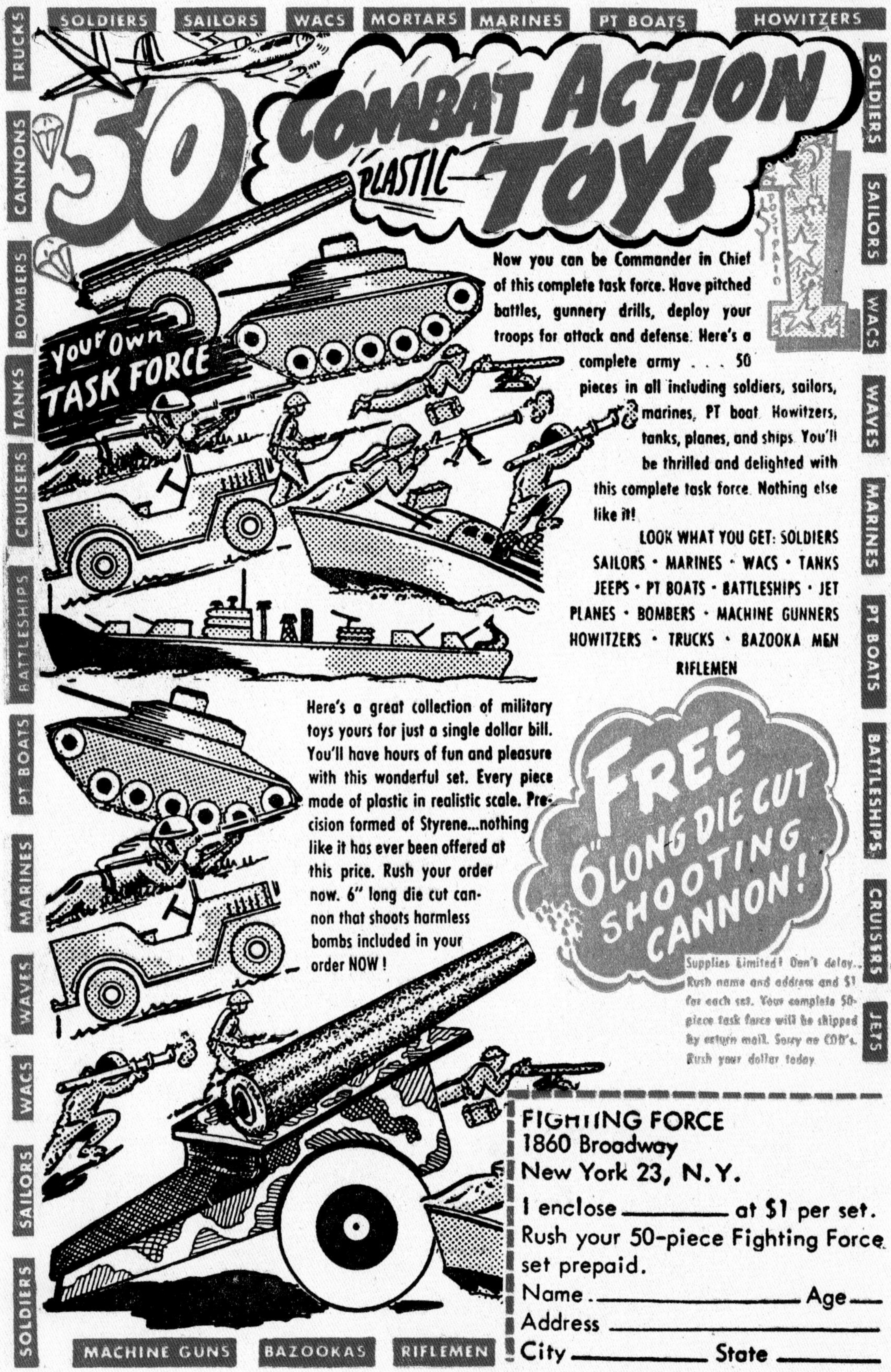
SOLDIERS
SAILORS
WACS
MORTARS
MARINES
PT BOATS
HOWITZERS
50 COMBAT ACTION PLASTIC TOYS
$1 POSTPAID
Your Own TASK FORCE
Now you can be Commander in Chief of this complete task force. Have pitched battles, gunnery drills, deploy your troops for attack and defense. Here's a complete army . . . 50 pieces in all including soldiers, sailors, marines, PT boat Howitzers, tanks, planes, and ships. You'll be thrilled and delighted with this complete task force. Nothing else like it!
LOOK WHAT YOU GET: SOLDIERS SAILORS • MARINES • WACS • TANKS JEEPS • PT BOATS • BATTLESHIPS • JET PLANES • BOMBERS • MACHINE GUNNERS HOWITZERS • TRUCKS • BAZOOKA MEN RIFLEMEN
Here's a great collection of military toys yours for just a single dollar bill. You'll have hours of fun and pleasure with this wonderful set. Every piece made of plastic in realistic scale. Precision formed of Styrene...nothing like it has ever been offered at this price. Rush your order now. 6" long die cut cannon that shoots harmless bombs included in your order NOW!
FREE 6" LONG DIE CUT SHOOTING CANNON!
Supplies Limited! Don't delay.. Rush name and address and $1 for each set. Your complete 50-piece task force will be shipped by return mail. Sorry no COD's. Rush your dollar today
FIGHTING FORCE
1860 Broadway
New York 23, N.Y.
I enclose ______ at $1 per set.
Rush your 50-piece Fighting Force set prepaid.
Name ______ Age ___
Address ______
City ______ State ______
MACHINE GUNS
BAZOOKAS
RIFLEMEN
TRUCKS
CANNONS
BOMBERS
TANKS
CRUISERS
BATTLESHIPS
PT BOATS
MARINES
WAVES
WACS
SAILORS
SOLDIERS
SOLDIERS
SAILORS
WACS
WAVES
MARINES
PT BOATS
BATTLESHIPS
CRUISERS
JETS

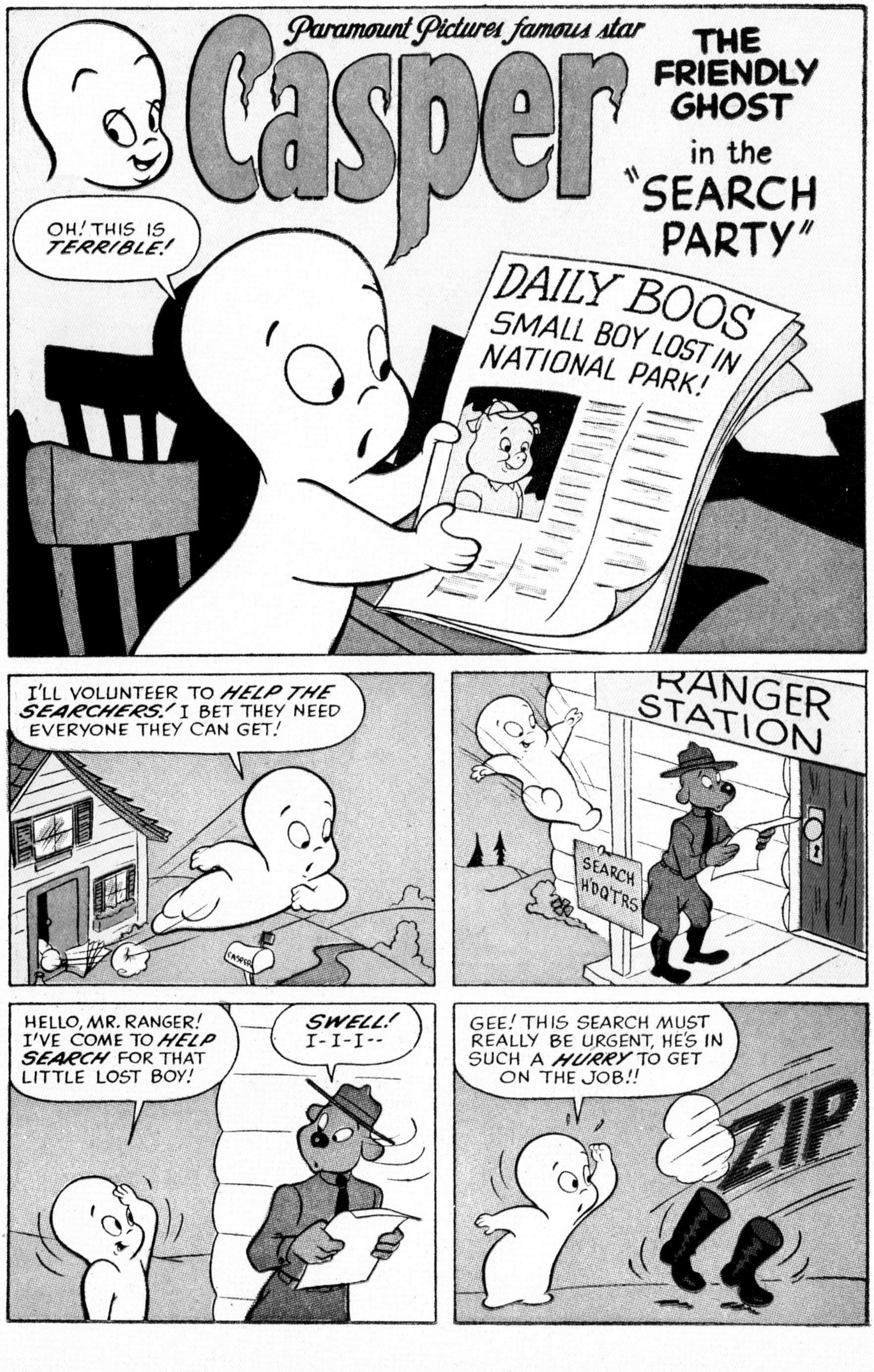
Paramount Pictures famous star
Casper
THE FRIENDLY GHOST
in the "SEARCH PARTY"
OH! THIS IS TERRIBLE!
DAILY BOOS
SMALL BOY LOST IN NATIONAL PARK!
I'LL VOLUNTEER TO HELP THE SEARCHERS! I BET THEY NEED EVERYONE THEY CAN GET!
CASPER
RANGER STATION
SEARCH HDQT'RS
HELLO, MR. RANGER! I'VE COME TO HELP SEARCH FOR THAT LITTLE LOST BOY!
SWELL! I-I-I--
GEE! THIS SEARCH MUST REALLY BE URGENT, HE'S IN SUCH A HURRY TO GET ON THE JOB!!
ZIP

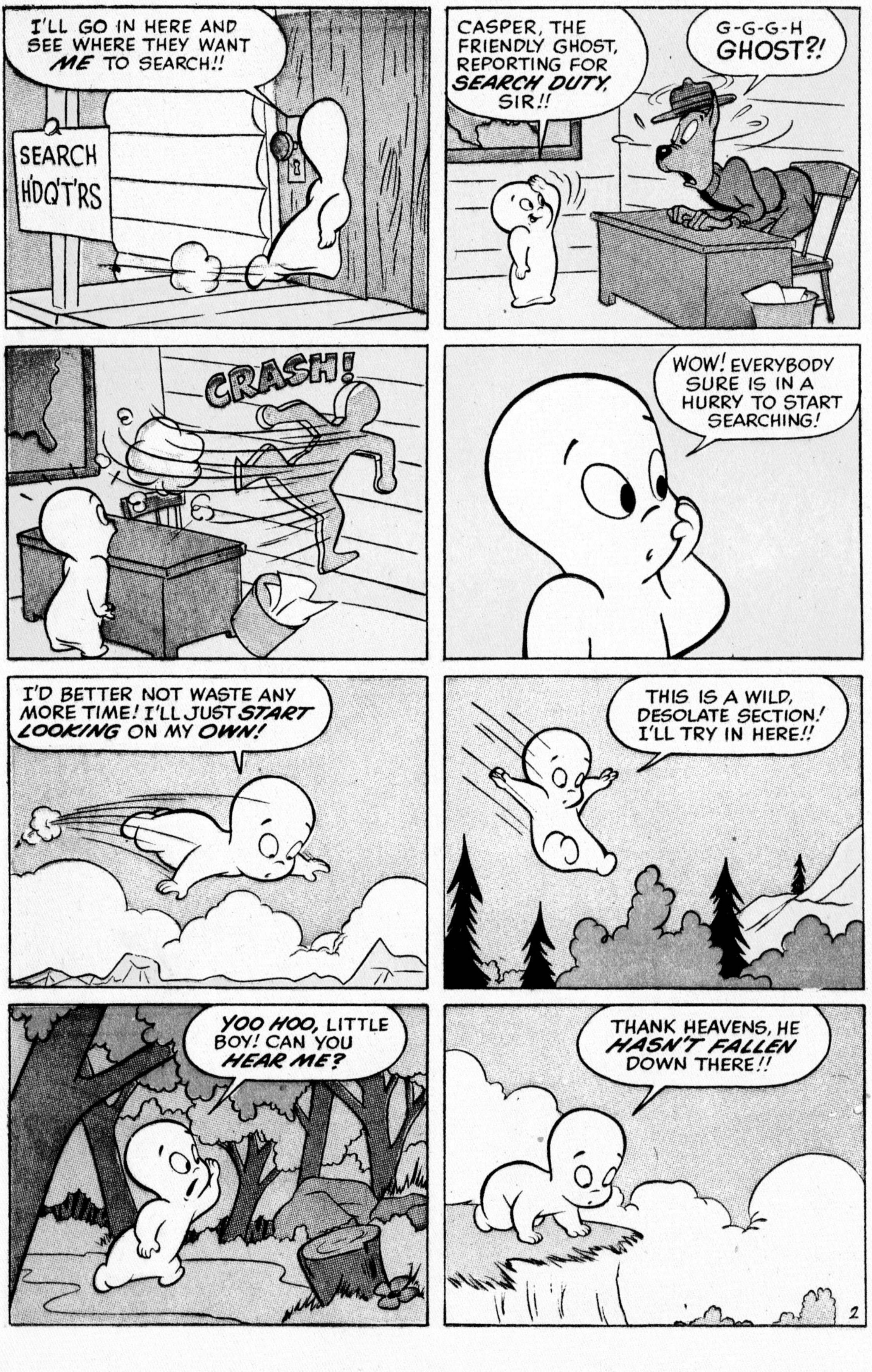

I'LL GO IN HERE AND SEE WHERE THEY WANT ME TO SEARCH!!
SEARCH H'DQ'T'RS
CASPER, THE FRIENDLY GHOST, REPORTING FOR SEARCH DUTY, SIR!!
G-G-G-H GHOST?!
CRASH!
WOW! EVERYBODY SURE IS IN A HURRY TO START SEARCHING!
I'D BETTER NOT WASTE ANY MORE TIME! I'LL JUST START LOOKING ON MY OWN!
THIS IS A WILD, DESOLATE SECTION! I'LL TRY IN HERE!!
YOO HOO, LITTLE BOY! CAN YOU HEAR ME?
THANK HEAVENS, HE HASN'T FALLEN DOWN THERE!!
2

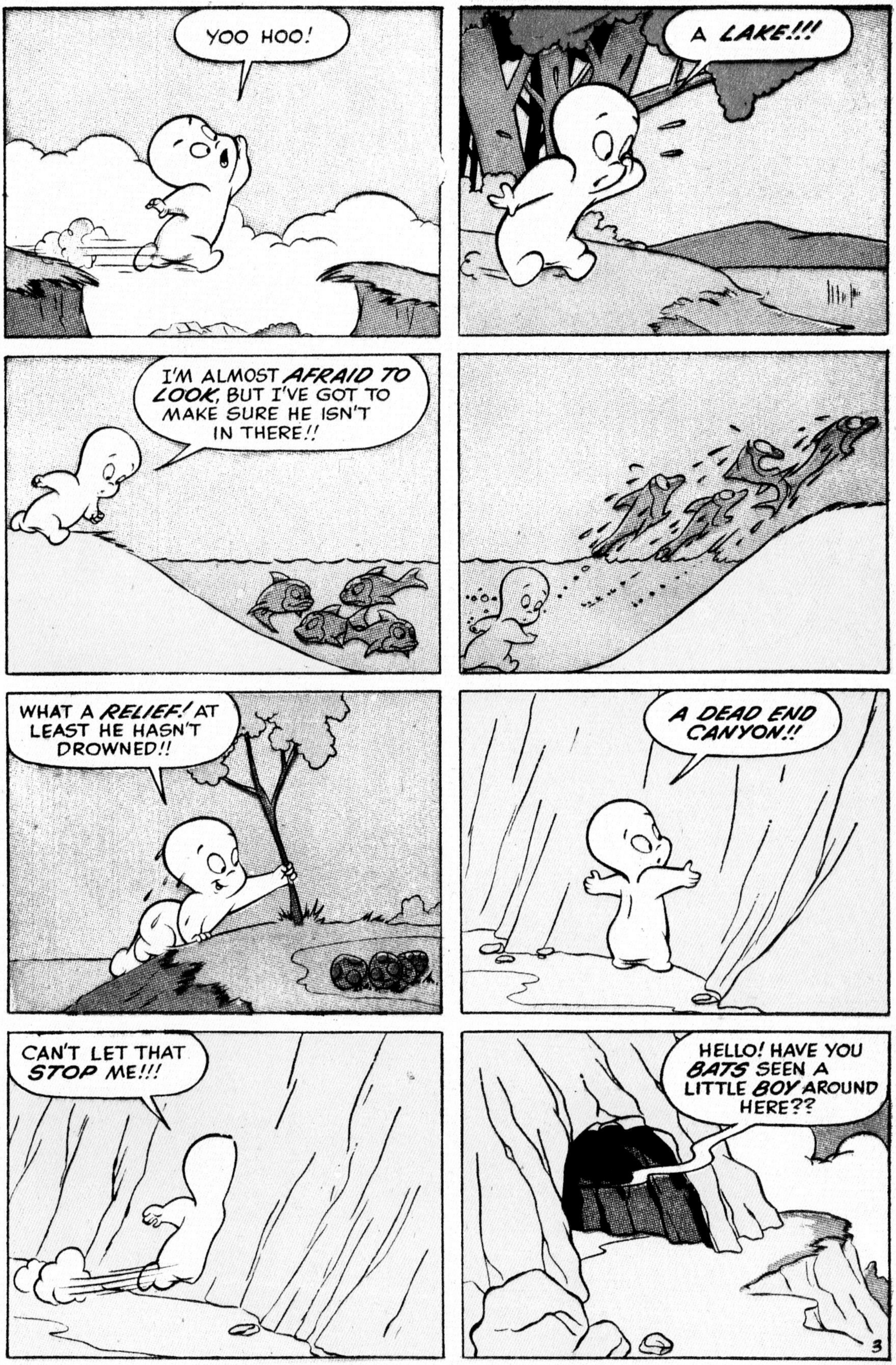
YOO HOO!
A LAKE!!!
I'M ALMOST AFRAID TO LOOK, BUT I'VE GOT TO MAKE SURE HE ISN'T IN THERE!!
WHAT A RELIEF! AT LEAST HE HASN'T DROWNED!!
A DEAD END CANYON!!
CAN'T LET THAT STOP ME!!!
HELLO! HAVE YOU BATS SEEN A LITTLE BOY AROUND HERE??
3

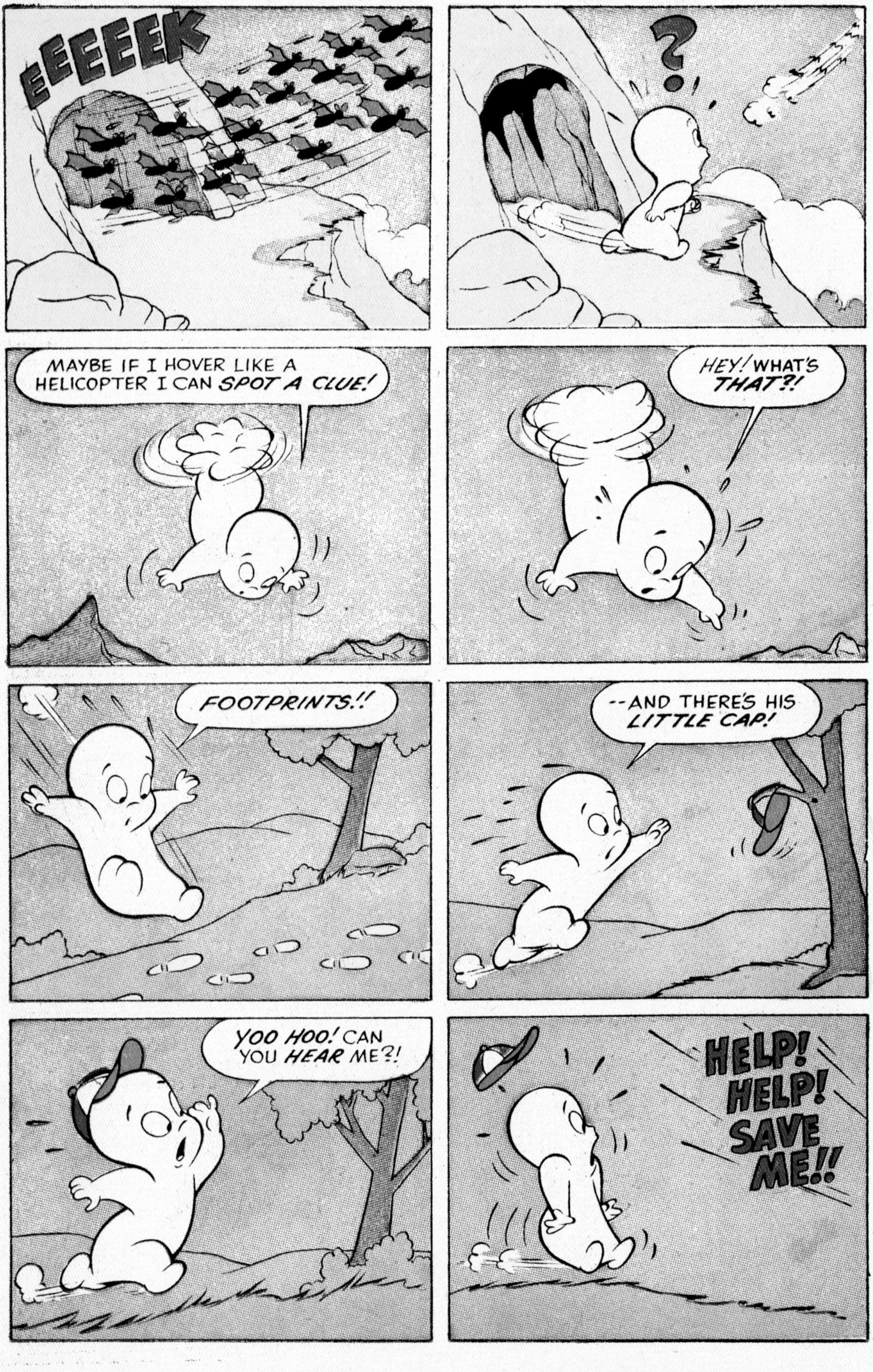
EEEEEK
?
MAYBE IF I HOVER LIKE A HELICOPTER I CAN SPOT A CLUE!
HEY! WHAT'S THAT?!
FOOTPRINTS!!
--AND THERE'S HIS LITTLE CAP!
YOO HOO! CAN YOU HEAR ME?!
HELP! HELP! SAVE ME!!

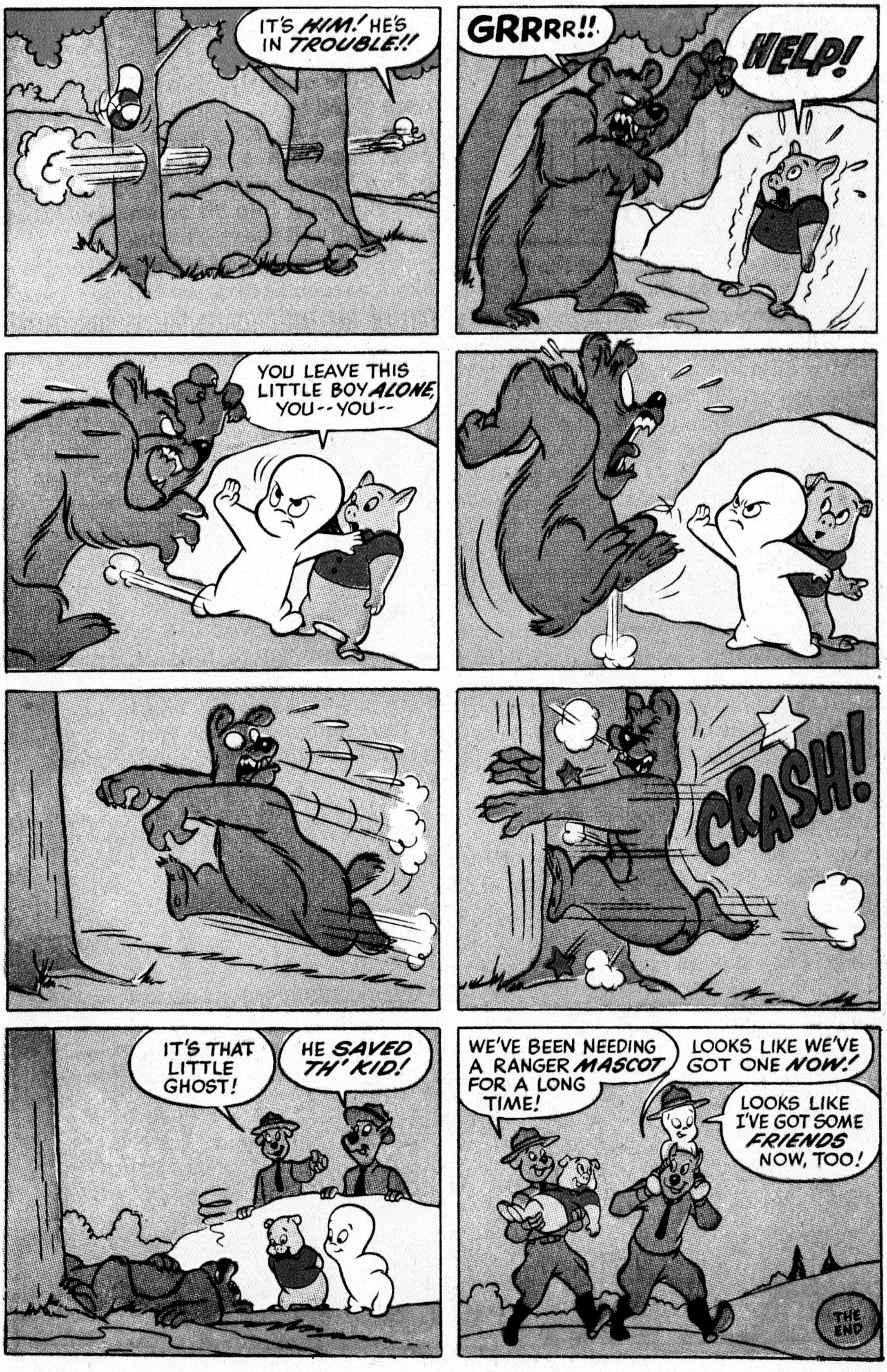
IT'S HIM! HE'S IN TROUBLE!!
GRRRR!!.
HELP!
YOU LEAVE THIS LITTLE BOY ALONE, YOU--YOU--
CRASH!
IT'S THAT LITTLE GHOST!
HE SAVED TH' KID!
WE'VE BEEN NEEDING A RANGER MASCOT FOR A LONG TIME!
LOOKS LIKE WE'VE GOT ONE NOW!
LOOKS LIKE I'VE GOT SOME FRIENDS NOW, TOO!
THE END

BOBBIT RABBIT

Bobbitt gazed longingly at the beautiful watermelon patch. "Oh, Mama!" he pleaded desperately. "Isn't there *some way* I can get at those watermelons?"

Mama Bunny glared at her son. "No!" she snapped. "I don't understand you, Bobbitt," she continued with a sigh. "In the first place, those watermelons belong to Farmer Black. *You* have no right to them! But in the second place, you're not supposed to *want* them! Whoever heard of a *rabbit eating watermelon?* The idea!" Still muttering and shaking her head, she dragged Bobbitt away from the farm.

The little rabbit went along, but his mind and his heart were still back in the watermelon patch. He longed with all his might and main to taste the luscious fruit! But so far he just hadn't been able to figure out a way to do it. Even if he could sneak into the watermelon patch itself—which he *had* managed to do once or twice—he still couldn't open the melons to get at the tempting pulp inside! Their strong green jackets were simply too hard for his little bunny teeth!

"OW!" Bobbitt tripped over something in the road, and sprawled flat on his face.

"Why don't you look where you're going?" scolded Mama Bunny, helping him to his feet.

Bobbitt scarcely heard her. His eyes were glued to the object he had tripped over—a *pen-knife,* an honest-to-goodness pen-knife—with a *real* blade! Swiftly, before Mama could see, he picked it up and slipped it into his pocket. His heart beat wildly all the way home.

He told no one of his plan. But that night, as soon as darkness fell, he slipped out of his bedroom window, and raced straight to Farmer Black's watermelon patch!

The pen-knife cut into the first melon easily. "Mmmmmmm!!" gurgled Bobbitt as he tasted the dripping, rosy fruit at last. "It's even *more* wonderful than I dreamed!" Greedily, he gobbled the whole melon. Then another . . . and another . . . and another . . .

He was on his fifth watermelon when Mama's voice hissed in his ear, "So! I *thought* I'd find you here, you rascal!" Bobbitt jumped to his feet, scattering melon seeds all over the ground. "Mama," he began—and stopped. Sharp pains tore at his tummy. His face turned a sickly green. The whole world spun around like a top!

"Mama . . ." Bobbitt's voice was very small. "I—I think I ate too many watermelons, Mama . . ."

Mama Bunny grabbed him before he fell. "Come on home, son!" she murmured gently. "I'll fix you up! And somehow, I don't think we'll be having any more watermelon troubles for a long, long time!"

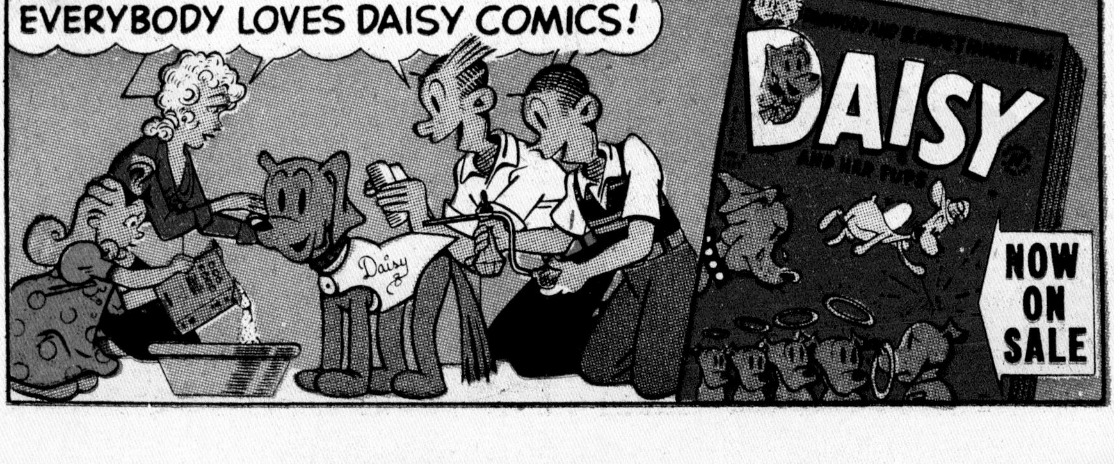
EVERYBODY LOVES DAISY COMICS!
Daisy
DAISY
NOW ON SALE

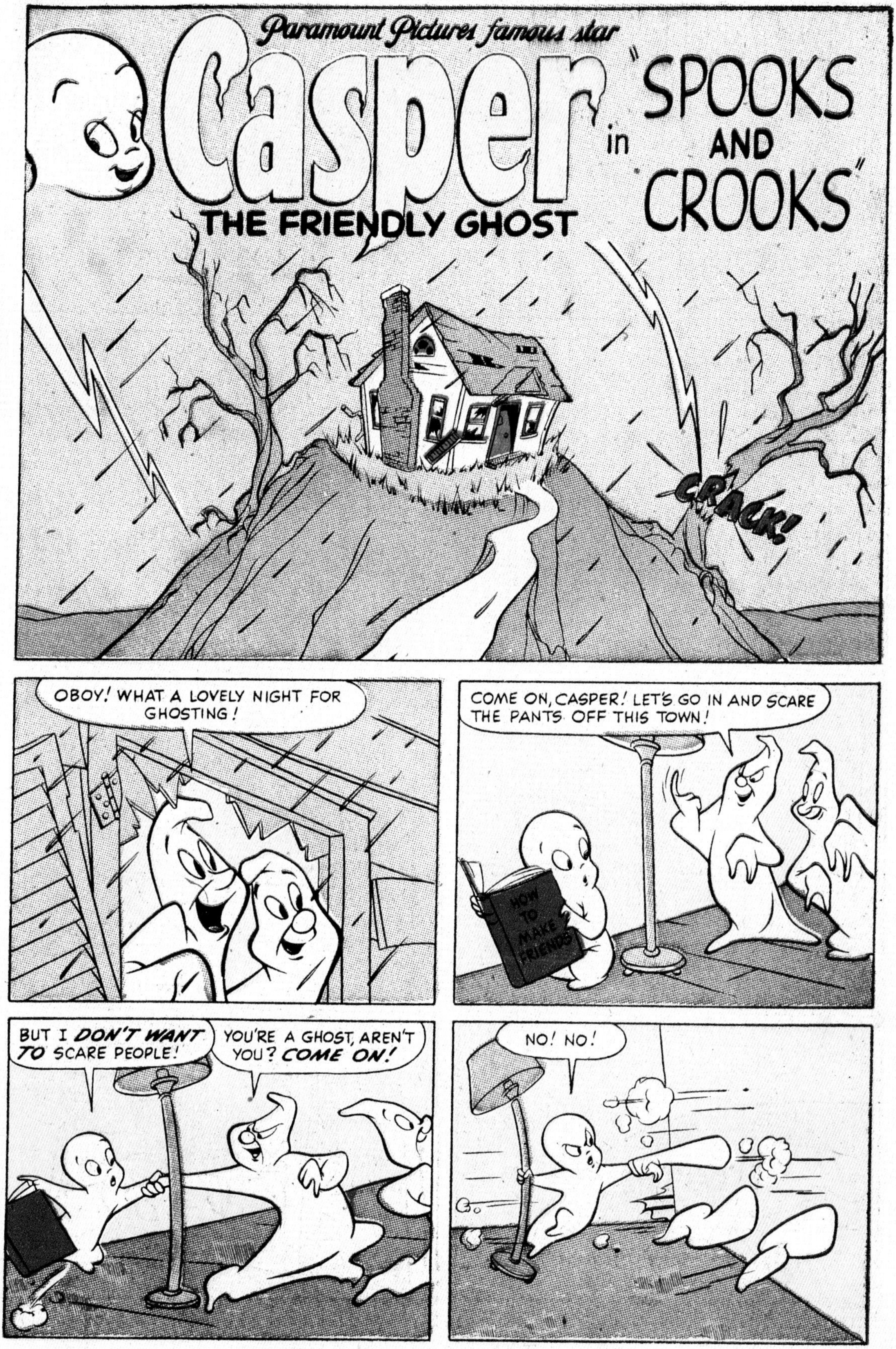
Paramount Pictures famous star
Casper THE FRIENDLY GHOST in "SPOOKS AND CROOKS"
CRACK!
OBOY! WHAT A LOVELY NIGHT FOR GHOSTING!
COME ON, CASPER! LET'S GO IN AND SCARE THE PANTS OFF THIS TOWN!
HOW TO MAKE FRIENDS
BUT I DON'T WANT TO SCARE PEOPLE!
YOU'RE A GHOST, AREN'T YOU? COME ON!
NO! NO!

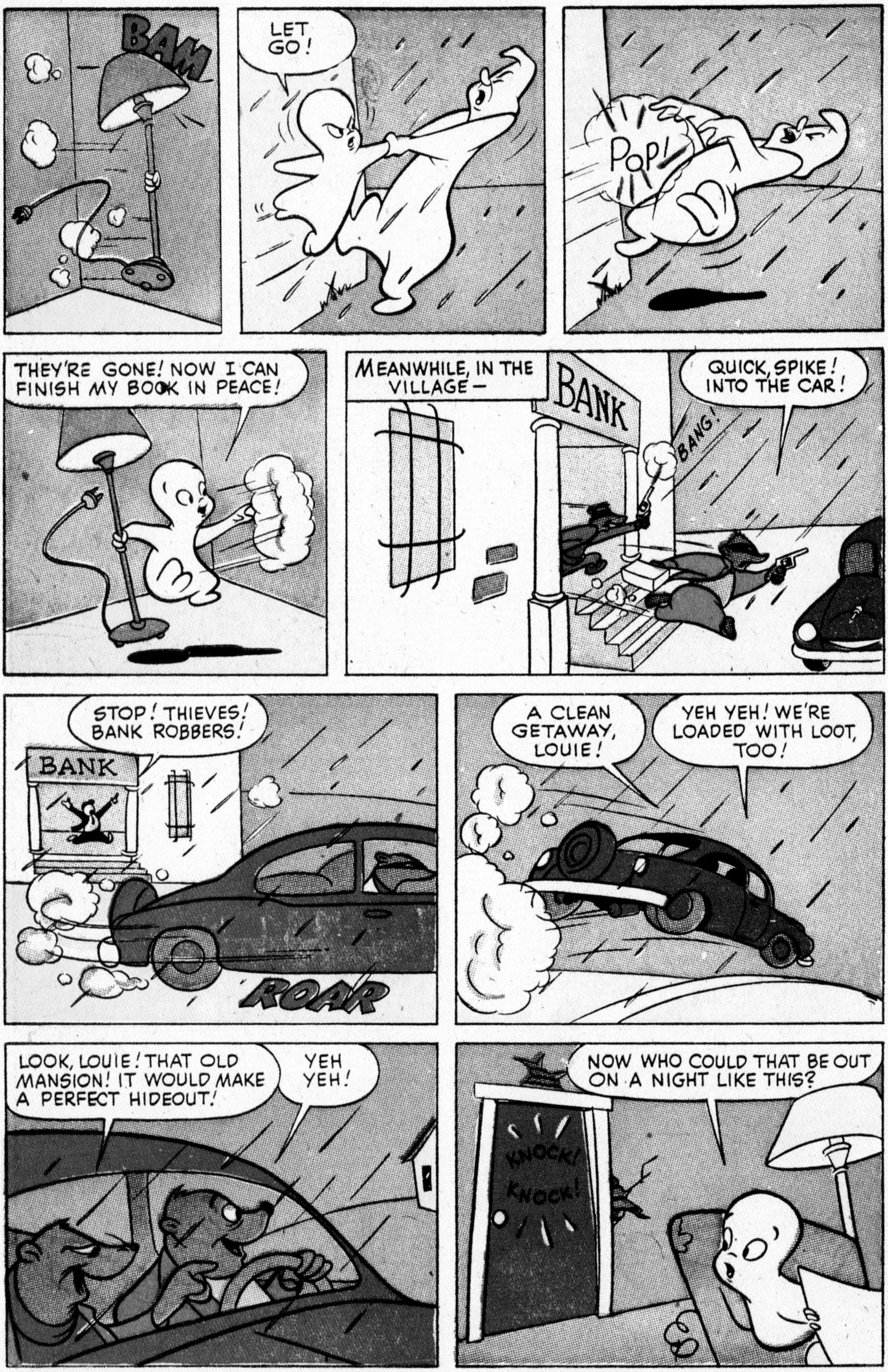
BAM
LET GO!
POP!
THEY'RE GONE! NOW I CAN FINISH MY BOOK IN PEACE!
MEANWHILE, IN THE VILLAGE—
BANK
BANG!
QUICK, SPIKE! INTO THE CAR!
BANK
STOP! THIEVES! BANK ROBBERS!
ROAR
A CLEAN GETAWAY, LOUIE!
YEH YEH! WE'RE LOADED WITH LOOT, TOO!
LOOK, LOUIE! THAT OLD MANSION! IT WOULD MAKE A PERFECT HIDEOUT!
YEH YEH!
KNOCK! KNOCK!
NOW WHO COULD THAT BE OUT ON A NIGHT LIKE THIS?

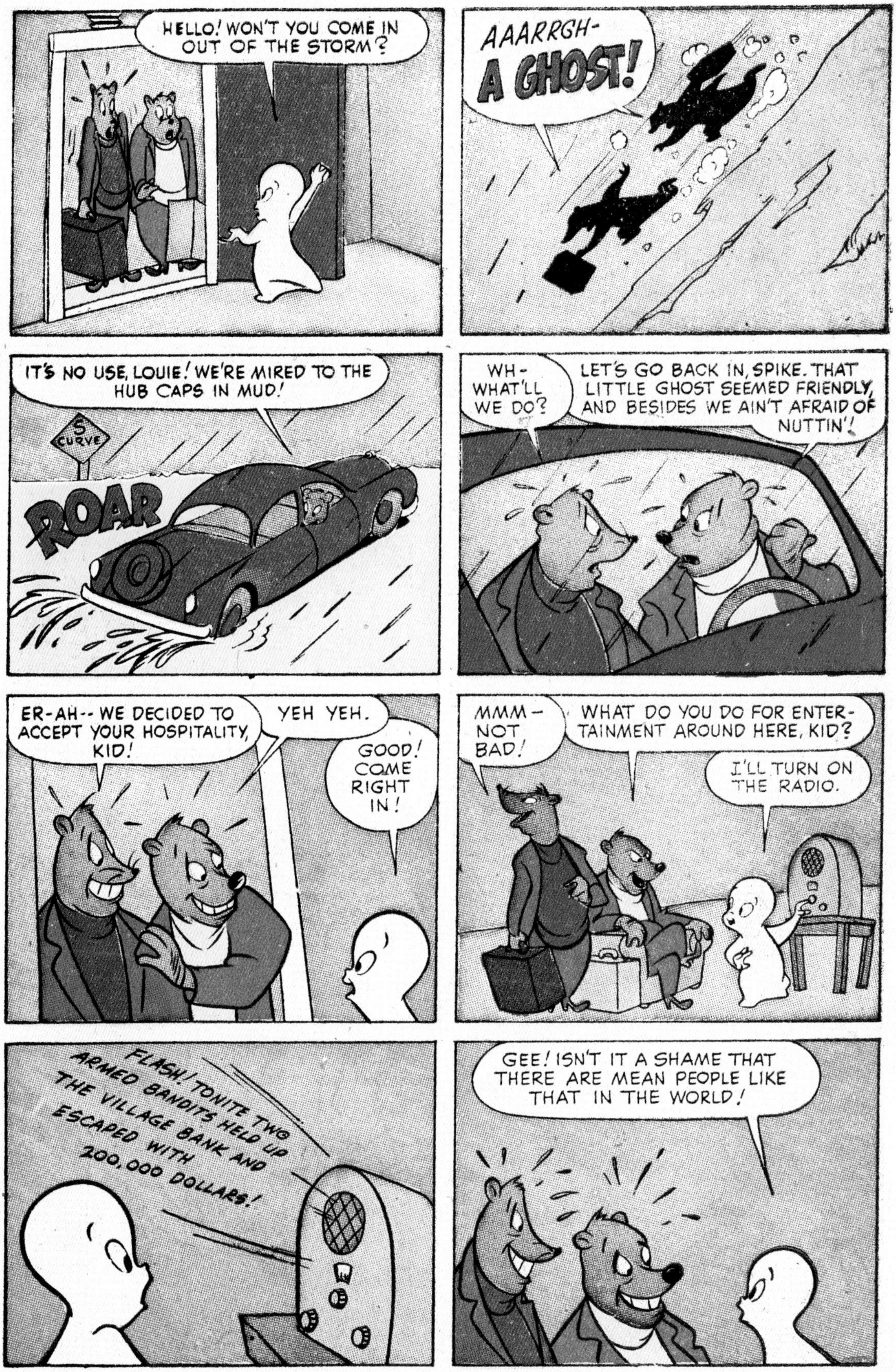
HELLO! WON'T YOU COME IN OUT OF THE STORM?
AAARRGH- A GHOST!
IT'S NO USE, LOUIE! WE'RE MIRED TO THE HUB CAPS IN MUD!
S CURVE
ROAR
WH- WHAT'LL WE DO?
LET'S GO BACK IN, SPIKE. THAT LITTLE GHOST SEEMED FRIENDLY, AND BESIDES WE AIN'T AFRAID OF NUTTIN'!
ER-AH-- WE DECIDED TO ACCEPT YOUR HOSPITALITY, KID!
YEH YEH.
GOOD! COME RIGHT IN!
MMM- NOT BAD!
WHAT DO YOU DO FOR ENTER-TAINMENT AROUND HERE, KID?
I'LL TURN ON THE RADIO.
FLASH! TONITE TWO ARMED BANDITS HELD UP THE VILLAGE BANK AND ESCAPED WITH 200,000 DOLLARS!
GEE! ISN'T IT A SHAME THAT THERE ARE MEAN PEOPLE LIKE THAT IN THE WORLD!

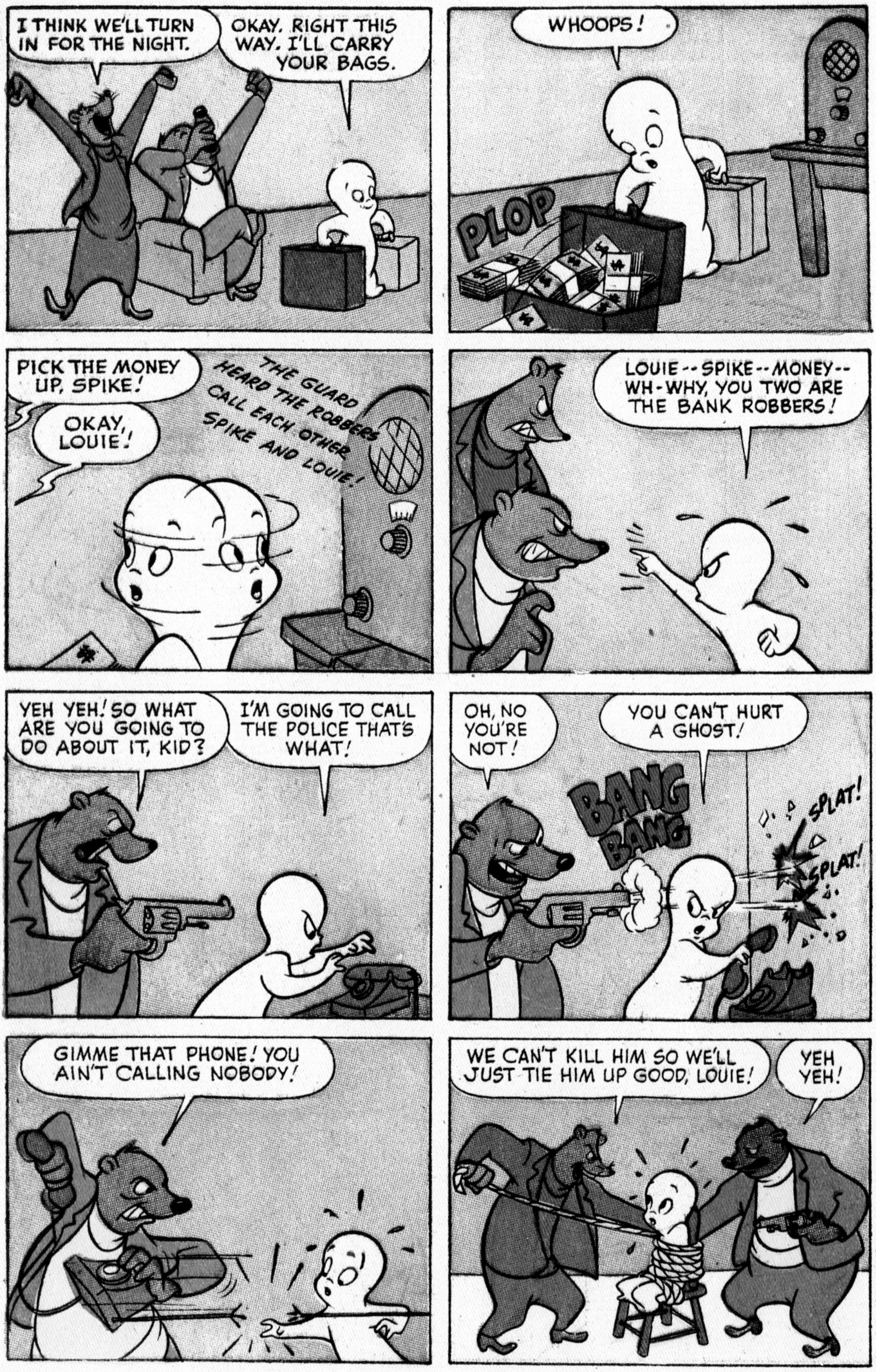

I THINK WE'LL TURN IN FOR THE NIGHT.
OKAY. RIGHT THIS WAY. I'LL CARRY YOUR BAGS.
WHOOPS!
PLOP
PICK THE MONEY UP, SPIKE!
OKAY, LOUIE!
THE GUARD HEARD THE ROBBERS CALL EACH OTHER SPIKE AND LOUIE!
LOUIE--SPIKE--MONEY--WH-WHY, YOU TWO ARE THE BANK ROBBERS!
YEH YEH! SO WHAT ARE YOU GOING TO DO ABOUT IT, KID?
I'M GOING TO CALL THE POLICE THAT'S WHAT!
OH, NO YOU'RE NOT!
YOU CAN'T HURT A GHOST!
BANG
BANG
SPLAT!
SPLAT!
GIMME THAT PHONE! YOU AIN'T CALLING NOBODY!
WE CAN'T KILL HIM SO WE'LL JUST TIE HIM UP GOOD, LOUIE!
YEH YEH!

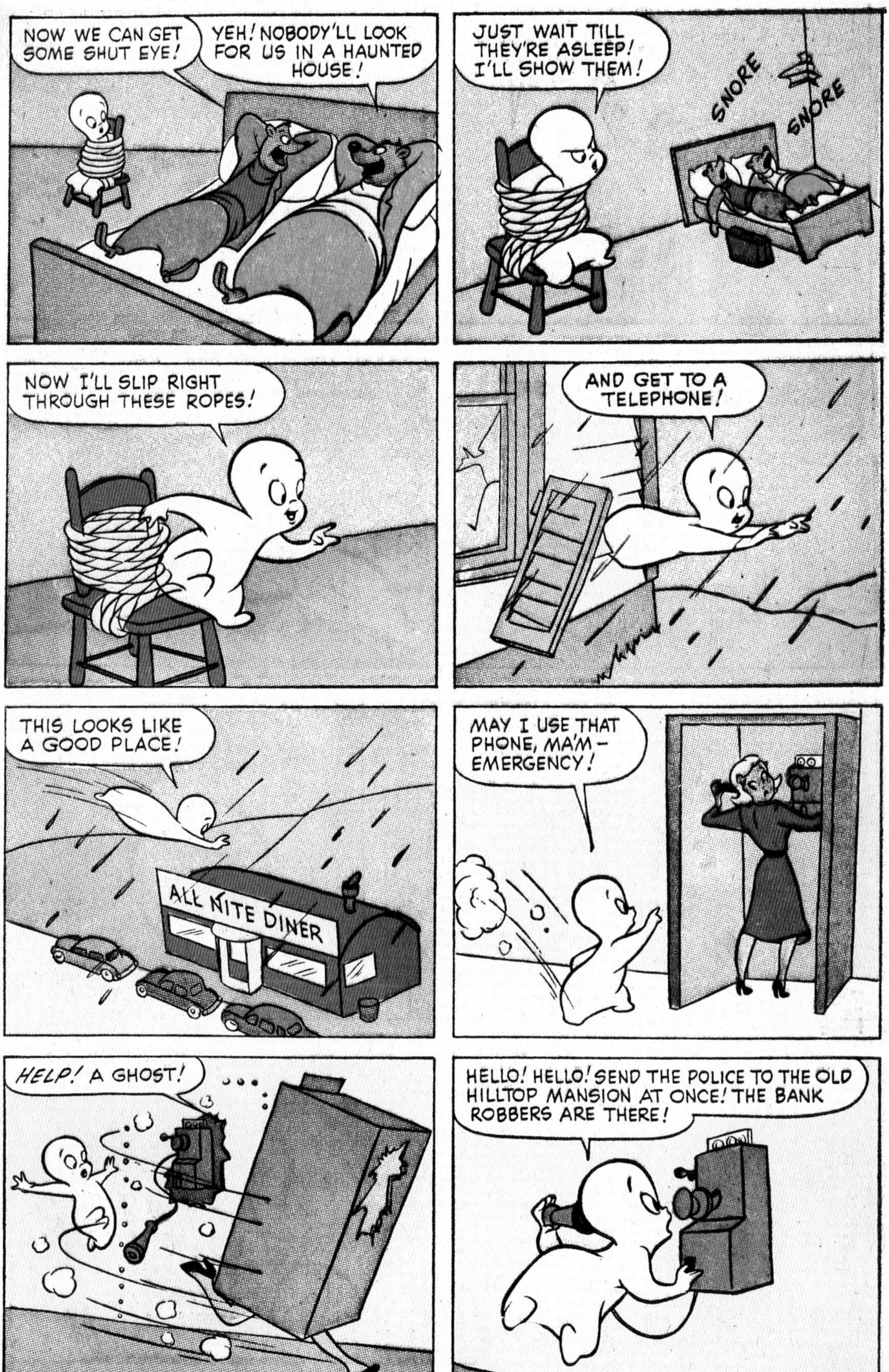
NOW WE CAN GET SOME SHUT EYE!
YEH! NOBODY'LL LOOK FOR US IN A HAUNTED HOUSE!
JUST WAIT TILL THEY'RE ASLEEP! I'LL SHOW THEM!
SNORE
SNORE
NOW I'LL SLIP RIGHT THROUGH THESE ROPES!
AND GET TO A TELEPHONE!
THIS LOOKS LIKE A GOOD PLACE!
ALL NITE DINER
MAY I USE THAT PHONE, MA'M - EMERGENCY!
HELP! A GHOST!
HELLO! HELLO! SEND THE POLICE TO THE OLD HILLTOP MANSION AT ONCE! THE BANK ROBBERS ARE THERE!

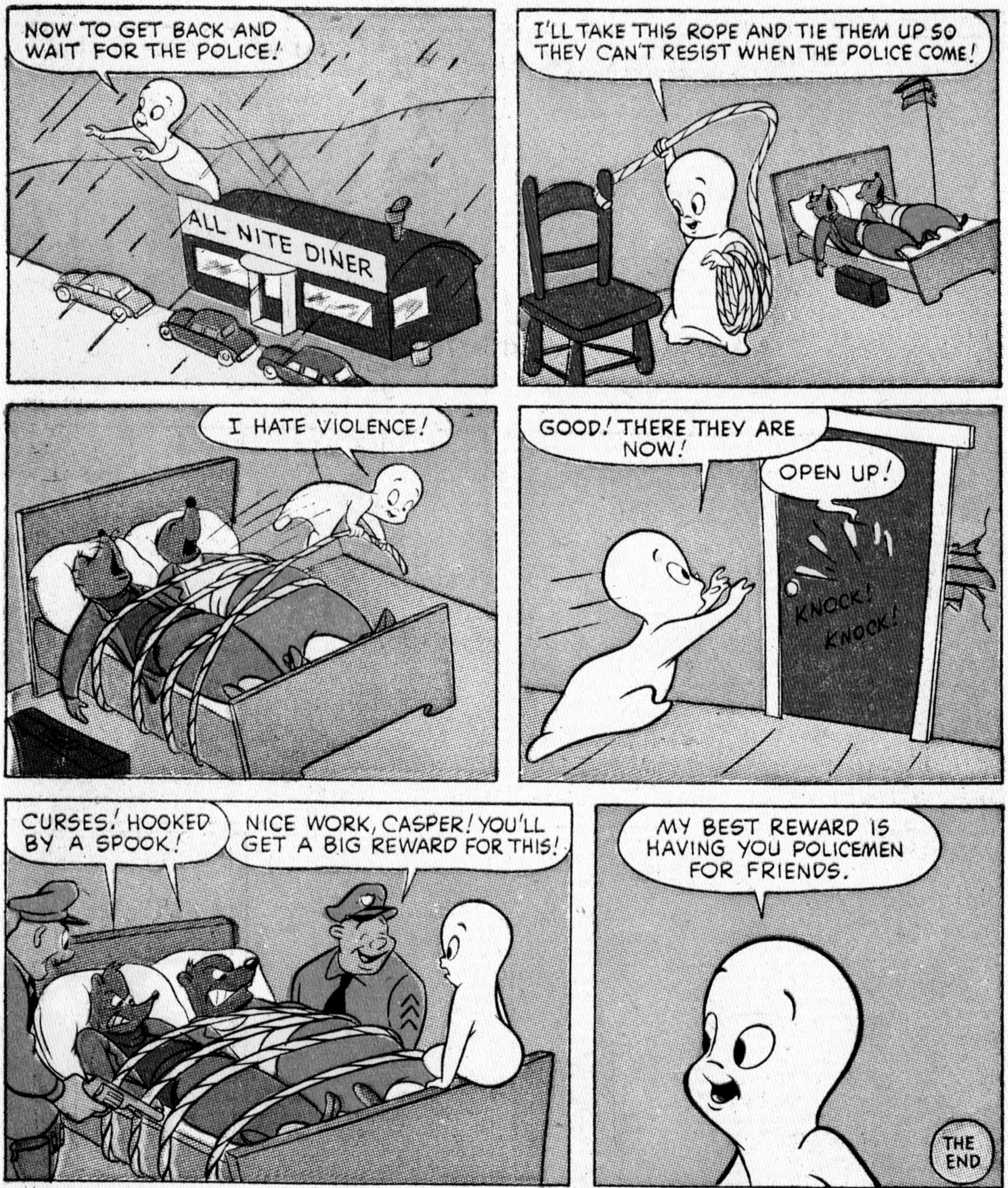
NOW TO GET BACK AND WAIT FOR THE POLICE!
ALL NITE DINER
I'LL TAKE THIS ROPE AND TIE THEM UP SO THEY CAN'T RESIST WHEN THE POLICE COME!
I HATE VIOLENCE!
GOOD! THERE THEY ARE NOW!
OPEN UP!
KNOCK! KNOCK!
CURSES! HOOKED BY A SPOOK!
NICE WORK, CASPER! YOU'LL GET A BIG REWARD FOR THIS!
MY BEST REWARD IS HAVING YOU POLICEMEN FOR FRIENDS.
THE END

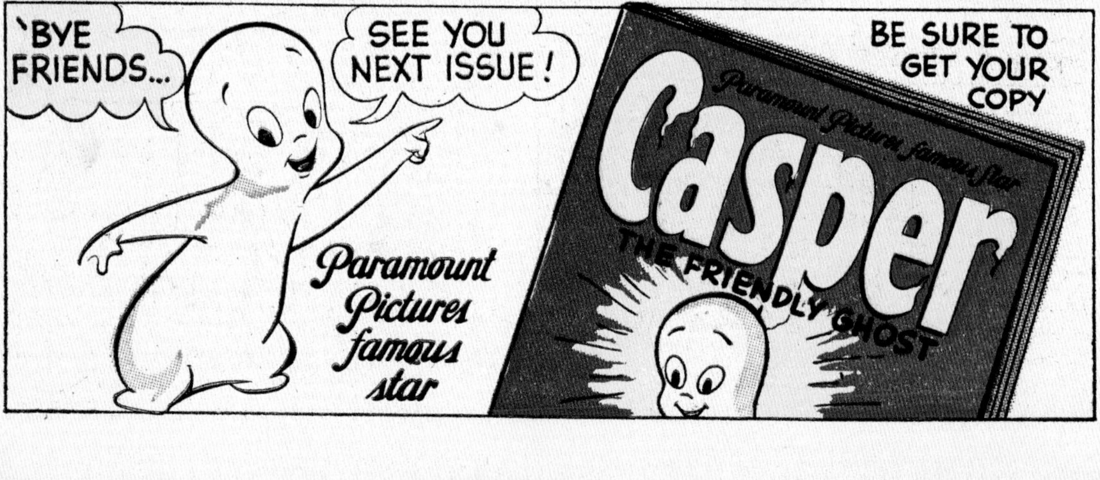
'BYE FRIENDS...
SEE YOU NEXT ISSUE!
Paramount Pictures famous star
BE SURE TO GET YOUR COPY
Paramount Pictures famous star
Casper
THE FRIENDLY GHOST

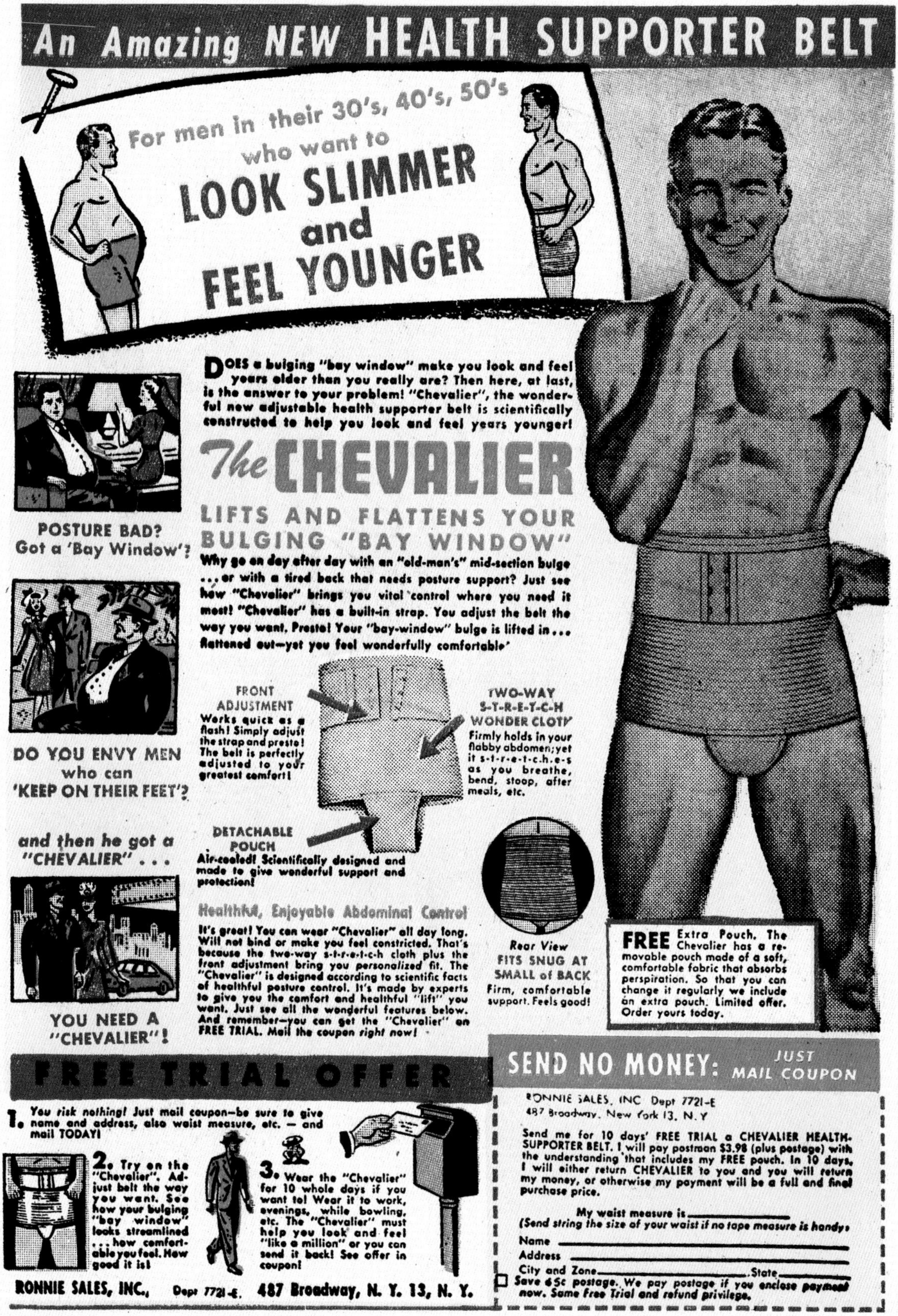

An Amazing NEW HEALTH SUPPORTER BELT
For men in their 30's, 40's, 50's who want to
LOOK SLIMMER and FEEL YOUNGER
DOES a bulging "bay window" make you look and feel years older than you really are? Then here, at last, is the answer to your problem! "Chevalier", the wonderful new adjustable health supporter belt is scientifically constructed to help you look and feel years younger!
The CHEVALIER
LIFTS AND FLATTENS YOUR BULGING "BAY WINDOW"
Why go on day after day with an "old-man's" mid-section bulge ... or with a tired back that needs posture support? Just see how "Chevalier" brings you vital control where you need it most! "Chevalier" has a built-in strap. You adjust the belt the way you want. Presto! Your "bay-window" bulge is lifted in ... flattened out—yet you feel wonderfully comfortable!
POSTURE BAD? Got a 'Bay Window'?
DO YOU ENVY MEN who can 'KEEP ON THEIR FEET'?
and then he got a "CHEVALIER" . . .
YOU NEED A "CHEVALIER"!
FRONT ADJUSTMENT
Works quick as a flash! Simply adjust the strap and presto! The belt is perfectly adjusted to your greatest comfort!
TWO-WAY S-T-R-E-T-C-H WONDER CLOTH
Firmly holds in your flabby abdomen; yet it s-t-r-e-t-c-h-e-s as you breathe, bend, stoop, after meals, etc.
DETACHABLE POUCH
Air-cooled! Scientifically designed and made to give wonderful support and protection!
Healthful, Enjoyable Abdominal Control
It's great! You can wear "Chevalier" all day long. Will not bind or make you feel constricted. That's because the two-way s-t-r-e-t-c-h cloth plus the front adjustment bring you personalized fit. The "Chevalier" is designed according to scientific facts of healthful posture control. It's made by experts to give you the comfort and healthful "lift" you want. Just see all the wonderful features below. And remember—you can get the "Chevalier" on FREE TRIAL. Mail the coupon right now!
Rear View
FITS SNUG AT SMALL of BACK
Firm, comfortable support. Feels good!
FREE Extra Pouch. The Chevalier has a removable pouch made of a soft, comfortable fabric that absorbs perspiration. So that you can change it regularly we include an extra pouch. Limited offer. Order yours today.
FREE TRIAL OFFER
1. You risk nothing! Just mail coupon—be sure to give name and address, also waist measure, etc. — and mail TODAY!
2. Try on the "Chevalier". Adjust belt the way you want. See how your bulging "bay window" looks streamlined ... how comfortable you feel. How good it is!
3. Wear the "Chevalier" for 10 whole days if you want to! Wear it to work, evenings, while bowling, etc. The "Chevalier" must help you look and feel "like a million" or you can send it back! See offer in coupon!
RONNIE SALES, INC., Dept 7721-E, 487 Broadway, N. Y. 13, N. Y.
SEND NO MONEY: JUST MAIL COUPON
RONNIE SALES, INC Dept 7721-E
487 Broadway, New York 13, N. Y
Send me for 10 days' FREE TRIAL a CHEVALIER HEALTH-SUPPORTER BELT. I will pay postman $3.98 (plus postage) with the understanding that includes my FREE pouch. In 10 days, I will either return CHEVALIER to you and you will return my money, or otherwise my payment will be a full and final purchase price.
My waist measure is
(Send string the size of your waist if no tape measure is handy)
Name
Address
City and Zone
State
Save 65c postage. We pay postage if you enclose payment now. Same Free Trial and refund privilege.

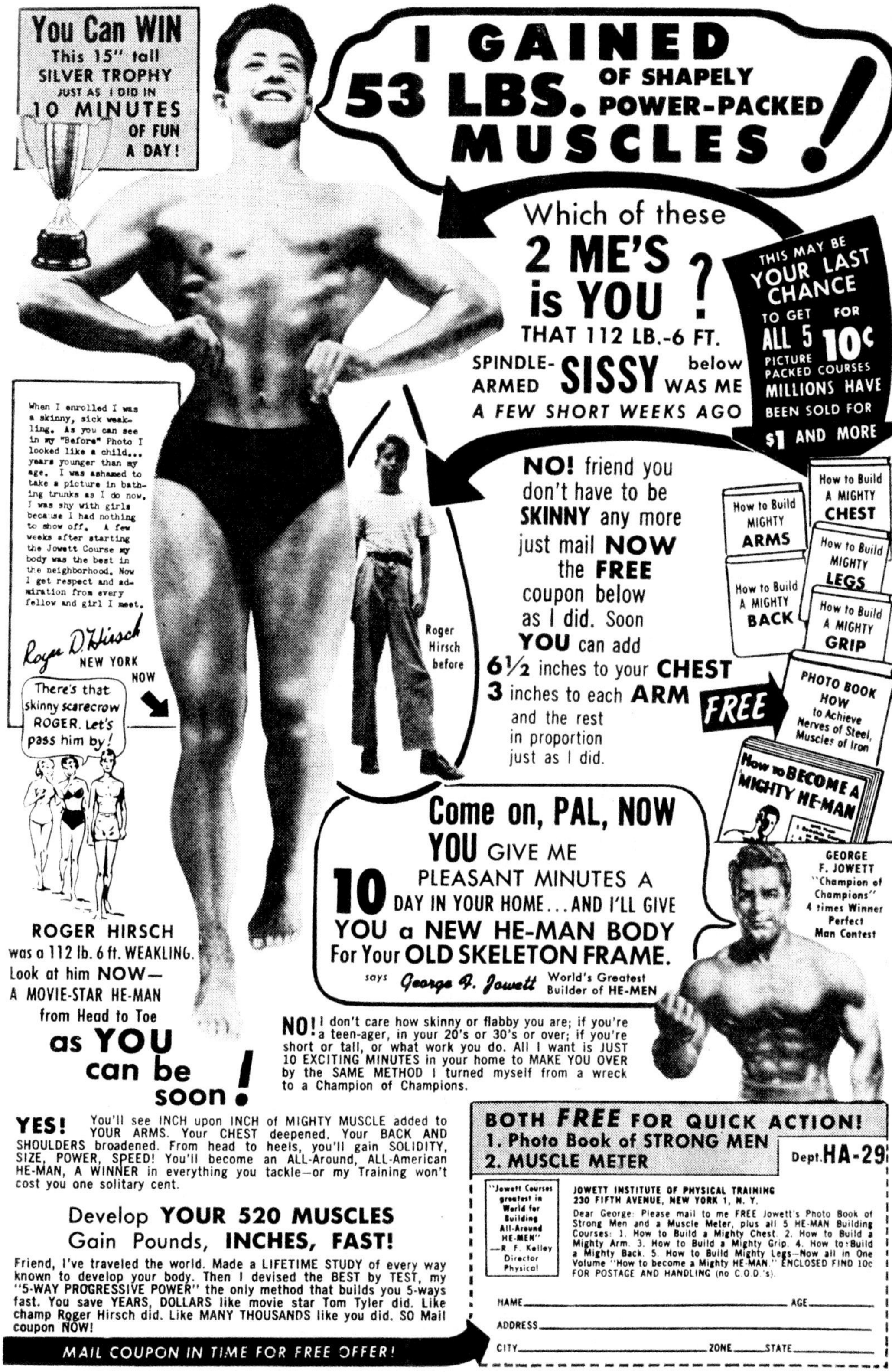

You Can WIN
This 15" tall
SILVER TROPHY
JUST AS I DID IN
10 MINUTES
OF FUN
A DAY!
I GAINED
53 LBS. OF SHAPELY POWER-PACKED
MUSCLES!
Which of these
2 ME'S
is YOU ?
THAT 112 LB.-6 FT.
SPINDLE-ARMED SISSY below WAS ME
A FEW SHORT WEEKS AGO
THIS MAY BE
YOUR LAST CHANCE
TO GET ALL 5 PICTURE PACKED COURSES FOR 10¢
MILLIONS HAVE BEEN SOLD FOR
$1 AND MORE
When I enrolled I was a skinny, sick weakling. As you can see in my "Before" Photo I looked like a child... years younger than my age. I was ashamed to take a picture in bathing trunks as I do now. I was shy with girls because I had nothing to show off. A few weeks after starting the Jowett Course my body was the best in the neighborhood. Now I get respect and admiration from every fellow and girl I meet.
Roger D. Hirsch
NEW YORK
NOW
There's that skinny scarecrow ROGER. Let's pass him by!
Roger Hirsch before
NO! friend you don't have to be SKINNY any more just mail NOW the FREE coupon below as I did. Soon YOU can add
6½ inches to your CHEST
3 inches to each ARM
and the rest in proportion just as I did.
How to Build MIGHTY ARMS
How to Build A MIGHTY CHEST
How to Build MIGHTY LEGS
How to Build A MIGHTY BACK
How to Build A MIGHTY GRIP
FREE
PHOTO BOOK HOW to Achieve Nerves of Steel, Muscles of Iron
How to BECOME A MIGHTY HE-MAN
Come on, PAL, NOW YOU GIVE ME 10 PLEASANT MINUTES A DAY IN YOUR HOME... AND I'LL GIVE YOU a NEW HE-MAN BODY For Your OLD SKELETON FRAME.
says George F. Jowett World's Greatest Builder of HE-MEN
GEORGE F. JOWETT
"Champion of Champions"
4 times Winner Perfect Man Contest
ROGER HIRSCH
was a 112 lb. 6 ft. WEAKLING.
Look at him NOW—
A MOVIE-STAR HE-MAN
from Head to Toe
as YOU can be soon!
NO! I don't care how skinny or flabby you are; if you're a teen-ager, in your 20's or 30's or over; if you're short or tall, or what work you do. All I want is JUST 10 EXCITING MINUTES in your home to MAKE YOU OVER by the SAME METHOD I turned myself from a wreck to a Champion of Champions.
YES! You'll see INCH upon INCH of MIGHTY MUSCLE added to YOUR ARMS. Your CHEST deepened. Your BACK AND SHOULDERS broadened. From head to heels, you'll gain SOLIDITY, SIZE, POWER, SPEED! You'll become an ALL-Around, ALL-American HE-MAN, A WINNER in everything you tackle—or my Training won't cost you one solitary cent.
Develop YOUR 520 MUSCLES
Gain Pounds, INCHES, FAST!
Friend, I've traveled the world. Made a LIFETIME STUDY of every way known to develop your body. Then I devised the BEST by TEST, my "5-WAY PROGRESSIVE POWER" the only method that builds you 5-ways fast. You save YEARS, DOLLARS like movie star Tom Tyler did. Like champ Roger Hirsch did. Like MANY THOUSANDS like you did. SO Mail coupon NOW!
MAIL COUPON IN TIME FOR FREE OFFER!
BOTH FREE FOR QUICK ACTION!
1. Photo Book of STRONG MEN
2. MUSCLE METER
Dept. HA-29
"Jowett Courses greatest in World for Building All-Around HE-MEN" —R. F. Kelley Director Physical
JOWETT INSTITUTE OF PHYSICAL TRAINING
230 FIFTH AVENUE, NEW YORK 1, N. Y.
Dear George: Please mail to me FREE Jowett's Photo Book of Strong Men and a Muscle Meter, plus all 5 HE-MAN Building Courses: 1. How to Build a Mighty Chest. 2. How to Build a Mighty Arm. 3. How to Build a Mighty Grip. 4. How to Build a Mighty Back. 5. How to Build Mighty Legs—Now all in One Volume "How to become a Mighty HE-MAN." ENCLOSED FIND 10c FOR POSTAGE AND HANDLING (no C.O.D.'s).
NAME
AGE
ADDRESS
CITY
ZONE
STATE

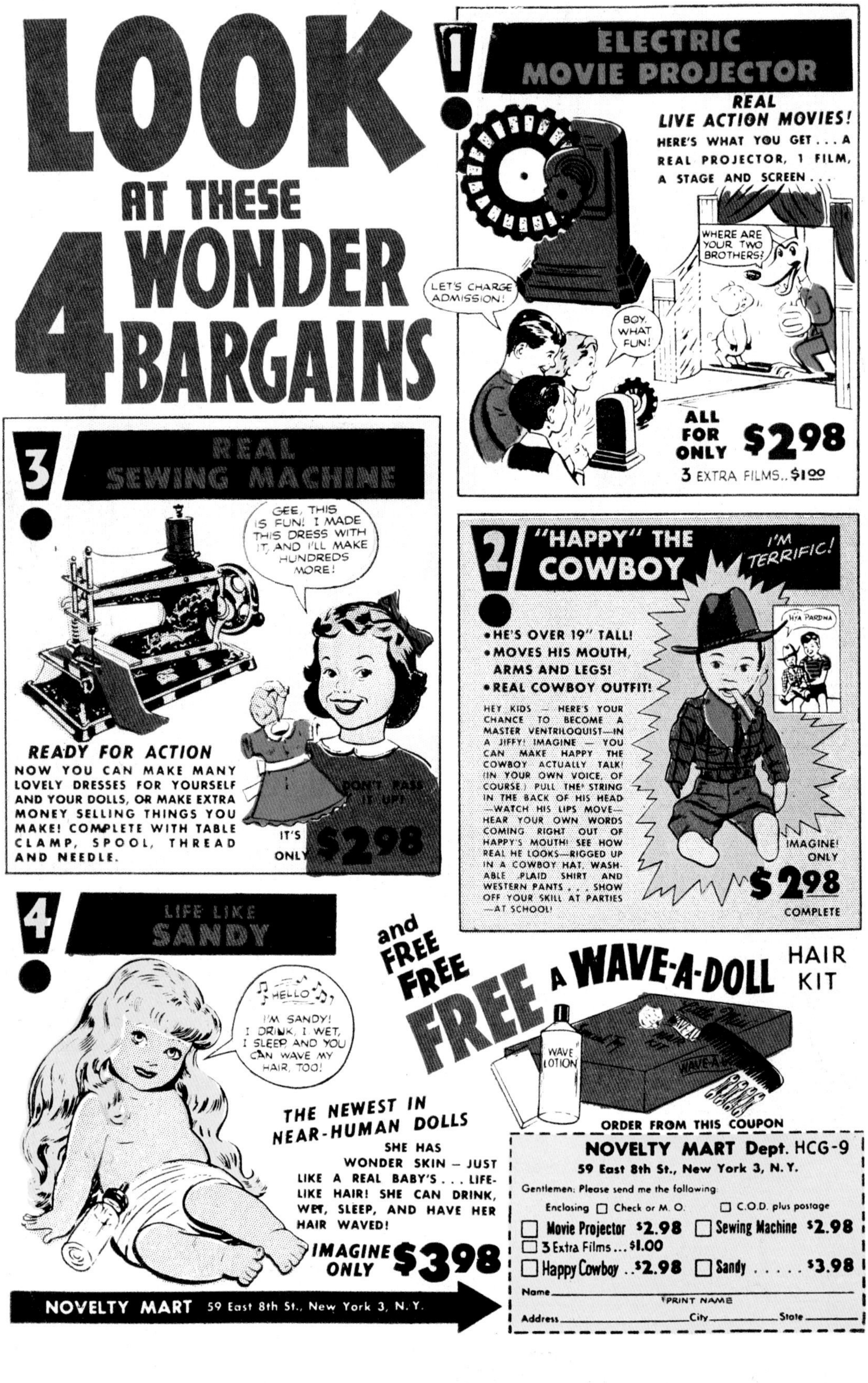
LOOK AT THESE 4 WONDER BARGAINS
1 ELECTRIC MOVIE PROJECTOR
REAL LIVE ACTION MOVIES!
HERE'S WHAT YOU GET . . . A REAL PROJECTOR, 1 FILM, A STAGE AND SCREEN . . .
WHERE ARE YOUR TWO BROTHERS?
LET'S CHARGE ADMISSION!
BOY, WHAT FUN!
ALL FOR ONLY $2.98
3 EXTRA FILMS.. $1.00
3 REAL SEWING MACHINE
GEE, THIS IS FUN! I MADE THIS DRESS WITH IT, AND I'LL MAKE HUNDREDS MORE!
READY FOR ACTION
NOW YOU CAN MAKE MANY LOVELY DRESSES FOR YOURSELF AND YOUR DOLLS, OR MAKE EXTRA MONEY SELLING THINGS YOU MAKE! COMPLETE WITH TABLE CLAMP, SPOOL, THREAD AND NEEDLE.
DON'T PASS IT UP!
IT'S ONLY $2.98
2 "HAPPY" THE COWBOY
I'M TERRIFIC!
HYA PARDNA
• HE'S OVER 19" TALL!
• MOVES HIS MOUTH, ARMS AND LEGS!
• REAL COWBOY OUTFIT!
HEY KIDS — HERE'S YOUR CHANCE TO BECOME A MASTER VENTRILOQUIST—IN A JIFFY! IMAGINE — YOU CAN MAKE HAPPY THE COWBOY ACTUALLY TALK! (IN YOUR OWN VOICE, OF COURSE.) PULL THE STRING IN THE BACK OF HIS HEAD —WATCH HIS LIPS MOVE— HEAR YOUR OWN WORDS COMING RIGHT OUT OF HAPPY'S MOUTH! SEE HOW REAL HE LOOKS—RIGGED UP IN A COWBOY HAT, WASHABLE PLAID SHIRT AND WESTERN PANTS . . . SHOW OFF YOUR SKILL AT PARTIES —AT SCHOOL!
IMAGINE! ONLY $2.98 COMPLETE
4 LIFE LIKE SANDY
HELLO
I'M SANDY! I DRINK, I WET, I SLEEP, AND YOU CAN WAVE MY HAIR, TOO!
and FREE FREE FREE A WAVE-A-DOLL HAIR KIT
WAVE LOTION
THE NEWEST IN NEAR-HUMAN DOLLS
SHE HAS WONDER SKIN — JUST LIKE A REAL BABY'S . . . LIFE-LIKE HAIR! SHE CAN DRINK, WET, SLEEP, AND HAVE HER HAIR WAVED!
IMAGINE ONLY $3.98
NOVELTY MART 59 East 8th St., New York 3, N.Y.
ORDER FROM THIS COUPON
NOVELTY MART Dept. HCG-9
59 East 8th St., New York 3, N.Y.
Gentlemen: Please send me the following:
Enclosing ☐ Check or M. O. ☐ C.O.D. plus postage
☐ Movie Projector $2.98 ☐ Sewing Machine $2.98
☐ 3 Extra Films ... $1.00
☐ Happy Cowboy .. $2.98 ☐ Sandy $3.98
Name ____ PRINT NAME
Address ____ City ____ State ____

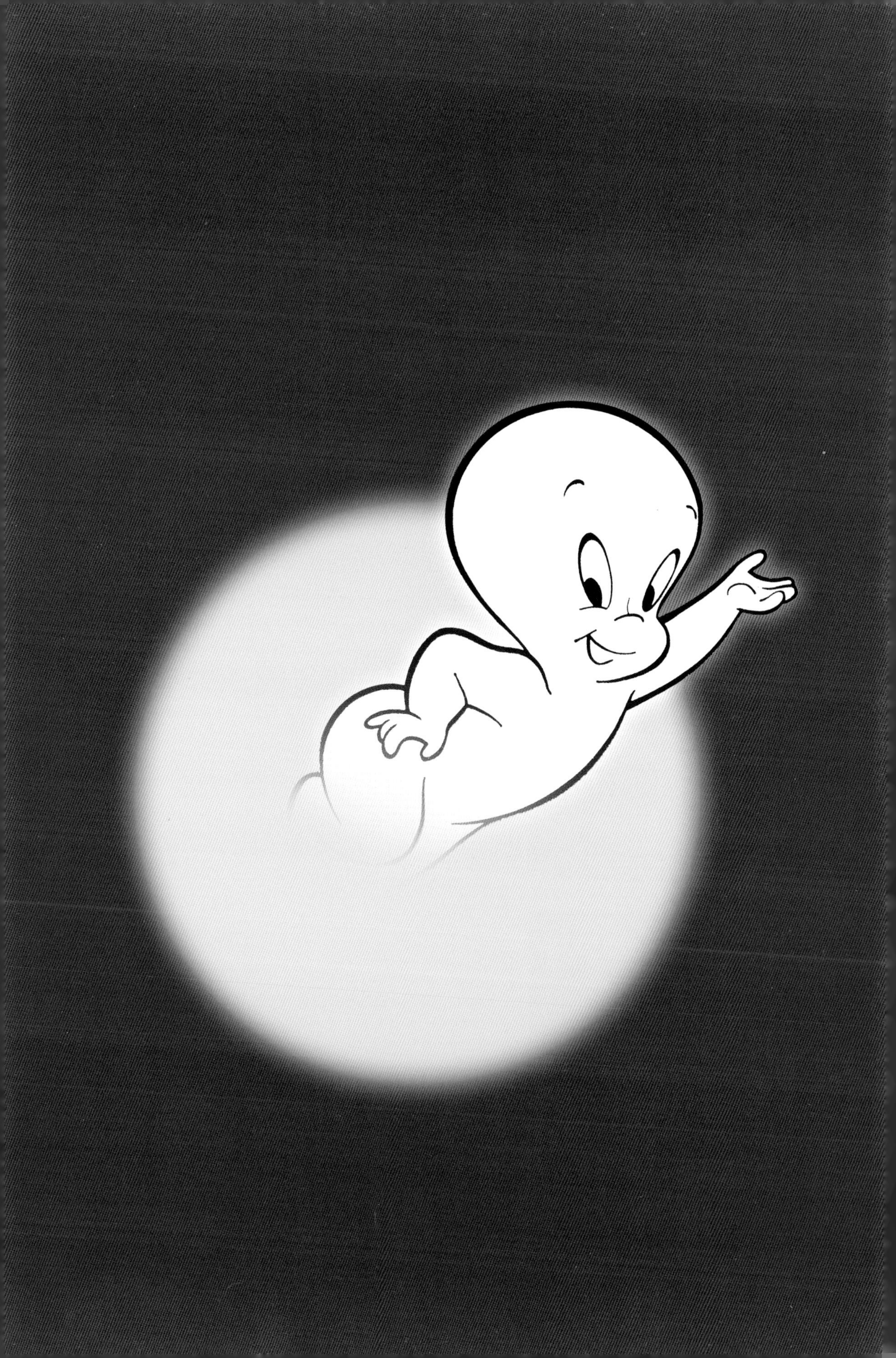

More Harvey Classics from Dark Horse

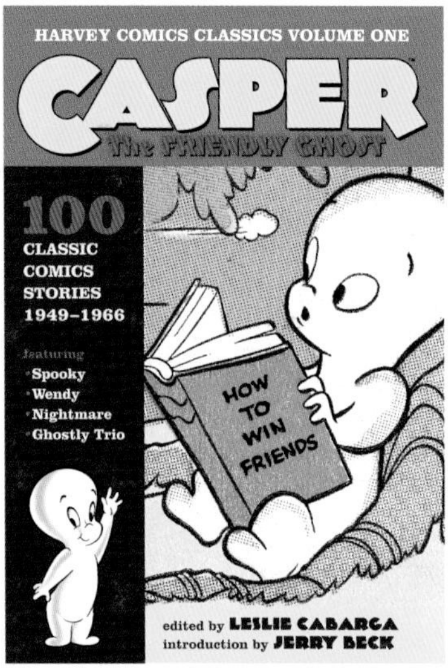
HARVEY COMICS CLASSICS VOLUME ONE
CASPER
The FRIENDLY GHOST
100
CLASSIC
COMICS
STORIES
1949–1966
featuring
Spooky
Wendy
Nightmare
Ghostly Trio
HOW TO WIN FRIENDS
edited by LESLIE CABARGA
introduction by JERRY BECK

It's amazing how many comics fans who grew up admiring Spider-Man, Batman, and Nick Fury still retain warm places in their hearts for Casper the Friendly Ghost. Now Dark Horse is delighted to participate in the revival of Casper, who remains among the most beloved of cartoon and comic-book icons. *Harvey Comics Classics Volume 1: Casper* contains over one hundred of Casper's very best stories, from the beginning of the Harvey series in 1952 through the classic years of the mid-1960s.

ISBN 978-1-59307-781-5

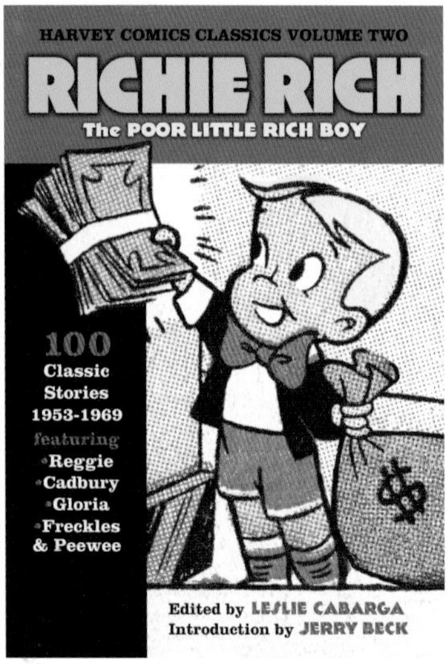
HARVEY COMICS CLASSICS VOLUME TWO
RICHIE RICH
The POOR LITTLE RICH BOY
100
Classic
Stories
1953-1969
featuring
Reggie
Cadbury
Gloria
Freckles
& Peewee
Edited by LESLIE CABARGA
Introduction by JERRY BECK

Move over, Uncle Scrooge! The richest character in comic-book history is about to get his due. Harvey Comics' original creation Richie Rich, the Poor Little Rich Boy, represented the fantasies of every comic-book-loving kid growing up in the 1960s and '70s. *Harvey Comics Classics Volume 2: Richie Rich* presents the ultimate tribute to the boy who has everything—and we do mean everything! This mega-compilation of the essential Richie collects his earliest and most substantial stories for the first time ever.

ISBN 978-1-59307-848-5

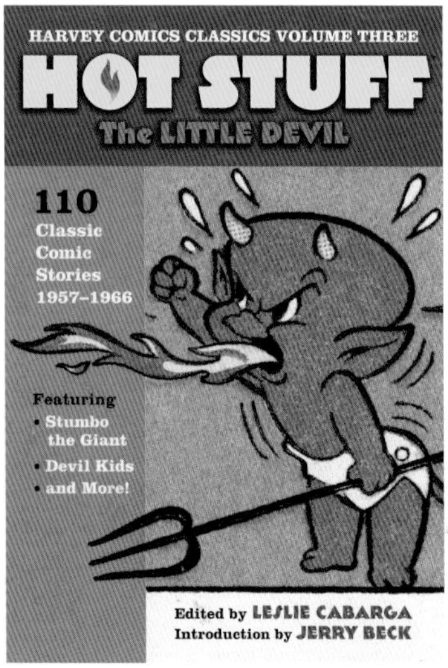
HARVEY COMICS CLASSICS VOLUME THREE
HOT STUFF
The LITTLE DEVIL
110
Classic
Comic
Stories
1957–1966
Featuring
Stumbo the Giant
Devil Kids
and More!
Edited by LESLIE CABARGA
Introduction by JERRY BECK

Who's the hotheaded little devil with a tail as pointed as his personality? It's Hot Stuff! This adorably mischievous imp has delighted comics fans since the 1950s, and this new collection sizzles with over one hundred of the funniest (and hottest!) classic Harvey Comics cartoons featuring Hot Stuff and his pals. *Harvey Comics Classics Volume 3: Hot Stuff* brings back the beautifully imaginative artwork, inspired humor, and long-out-of-print stories featuring the adventures of the sprightly little demon.

ISBN 978-1-59307-914-7

HARVEY COMICS CLASSICS VOLUME FOUR
BABY HUEY
The Baby Giant
500 LBS.
110
Classic
Comics
1949–1966
featuring
Papa Duck
The Fox!
Buzzy
Herman
& Katnip
Edited by LESLIE CABARGA Intro by JERRY BECK

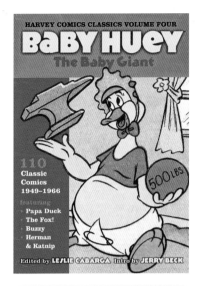

Oversized, oblivious, and oh-so-good-natured duckling Baby Huey first delighted audiences in 1949 when he appeared in the pages of *Casper the Friendly Ghost*, but he quickly lumbered his way into the bigger world of cartoons and his own comic-book series! Join Baby Huey, his lovingly baffled parents, and his duckling pals in this jumbo collection of classic stories of outsized adventures.

ISBN 978-1-59307-977-2

HARVEY COMICS CLASSICS VOLUME FIVE
The
HARVEY GIRLS
LITTLE AUDREY, LITTLE DOT & LITTLE LOTTA
125
Classic
Comic
Stories
1949–1966
Edited by LESLIE CABARGA
Introduction by JERRY BECK

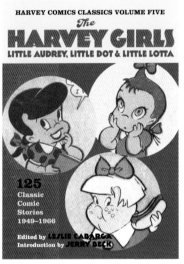

They're cute, they're clever, and they're obsessive! Some of Harvey Comics' biggest stars were three "little" girls with large dreams, enormous hearts, and king-size laughs: Little Audrey, Little Dot, and Little Lotta. Little Audrey's comic-book stories were filled with ingenuity, and her spunky, protofeminist antics rivaled those of her cartoon progenitor Little Lulu. The amusingly obsessive Little Dot and her unique coterie of eccentric aunts and uncles became the basis for some of the funniest stories in comic-book history. And Little Lotta has big fun with adventures showcasing an incredible strength that equaled her insatiable appetite!

ISBN 978-1-59582-171-3

$19.95
each!

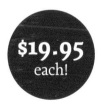

Find out more about these and other great Dark Horse all-ages titles at darkhorse.com!

AVAILABLE AT YOUR LOCAL COMICS SHOP OR BOOKSTORE

TO FIND A COMICS SHOP IN YOUR AREA, CALL 1-888-266-4226

For more information or to order direct: On the web: darkhorse.com • E-mail: mailorder@darkhorse.com
Phone: 1-800-862-0052 Mon.–Fri. 9 AM to 5 PM Pacific Time.